Cakes & Cobblers

Recipes to make your own gifts

Use these recipes to delight your friends and family. Each recipe includes gift tags for your convenience – just cut them out and personalize!

To decorate jars, cut fabric in 9" diameter circles. Screw down the jar ring to hold fabric in place or hold fabric with a ribbon, raffia, twine, yarn, lace, or string (first secure the fabric with a rubber band before tying). Punch a hole into the corner of the tag and use the ribbon, raffia, twine, yarn, lace, or string to attach the tag to the jar.

These gifts should keep for up to six months. If the mix contains nuts, it should be used within three months.

Printed in the United States of America
by G&R Publishing Co.

Distributed By:

507 Industrial Street
Waverly, IA 50677

ISBN 1-56383-164-3
Item #3010

Honey Cake Mix

1/2 C. chopped walnuts
3/4 C. raisins
1 1/2 tsp. baking soda
1 tsp. baking powder
2 tsp. cinnamon
1/2 tsp. ginger
3 C. flour

Layer the ingredients in the order given into a wide-mouth 1-quart canning jar. Pack each layer into place before adding the next ingredient.

Attach a gift tag with the mixing and baking instructions.

❋ Use a thin paper plate as a funnel for an easy and no mess way to add ingredients to the jar. ❋

Honey Cake

1 jar Honey Cake Mix
1 1/4 C. honey
3/4 C. vegetable oil
3/4 C. brewed coffee
2 tsp. vanilla
3 eggs
1/2 C. sugar
1/2 C. honey

Preheat oven to 350°F. In a saucepan, cook 1 1/4 cup honey, oil, coffee and vanilla, stirring gently until well blended. Set mixture aside to cool. In a medium bowl, beat eggs and sugar on high speed until thick and pale yellow. Beat the cooled honey mixture into the eggs. Add the Honey Cake Mix and beat until well blended. Scrape batter into a greased 9 x 13 inch pan. Bake for 35 to 40 minutes. As soon as cake is removed from oven use a fork to prick holes all over the surface. Heat 1/2 cup honey and gently pour over the top allowing to seep into cake. Allow cake to cool completely before cutting.

Honey Cake

1 jar Honey Cake Mix
1 1/4 C. honey
3/4 C. vegetable oil
3/4 C. brewed coffee

2 tsp. vanilla
3 eggs
1/2 C. sugar
1/2 C. honey

Preheat oven to 350°F. In a saucepan, cook 1 1/4 cup honey, oil, coffee and vanilla, stirring gently until well blended. Set mixture aside to cool. In a medium bowl, beat eggs and sugar on high speed until thick and pale yellow. Beat the cooled honey mixture into the eggs. Add the Honey Cake Mix and beat until well blended. Scrape batter into a greased 9 x 13 inch pan. Bake for 35 to 40 minutes. As soon as cake is removed from oven use a fork to prick holes all over the surface. Heat 1/2 cup honey and gently pour over the top allowing to seep into cake. Allow cake to cool completely before cutting.

Honey Cake

1 jar Honey Cake Mix
1 1/4 C. honey
3/4 C. vegetable oil
3/4 C. brewed coffee

2 tsp. vanilla
3 eggs
1/2 C. sugar
1/2 C. honey

Preheat oven to 350°F. In a saucepan, cook 1 1/4 cup honey, oil, coffee and vanilla, stirring gently until well blended. Set mixture aside to cool. In a medium bowl, beat eggs and sugar on high speed until thick and pale yellow. Beat the cooled honey mixture into the eggs. Add the Honey Cake Mix and beat until well blended. Scrape batter into a greased 9 x 13 inch pan. Bake for 35 to 40 minutes. As soon as cake is removed from oven use a fork to prick holes all over the surface. Heat 1/2 cup honey and gently pour over the top allowing to seep into cake. Allow cake to cool completely before cutting.

Honey Cake

1 jar Honey Cake Mix
1 1/4 C. honey
3/4 C. vegetable oil
3/4 C. brewed coffee

2 tsp. vanilla
3 eggs
1/2 C. sugar
1/2 C. honey

Preheat oven to 350°F. In a saucepan, cook 1 1/4 cup honey, oil, coffee and vanilla, stirring gently until well blended. Set mixture aside to cool. In a medium bowl, beat eggs and sugar on high speed until thick and pale yellow. Beat the cooled honey mixture into the eggs. Add the Honey Cake Mix and beat until well blended. Scrape batter into a greased 9 x 13 inch pan. Bake for 35 to 40 minutes. As soon as cake is removed from oven use a fork to prick holes all over the surface. Heat 1/2 cup honey and gently pour over the top allowing to seep into cake. Allow cake to cool completely before cutting.

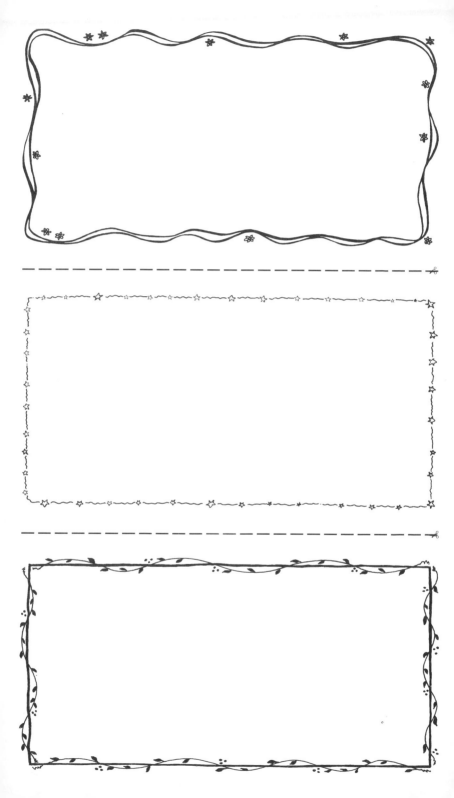

Honey Cake

1 jar Honey Cake Mix
1 1/4 C. honey
3/4 C. vegetable oil
3/4 C. brewed coffee

2 tsp. vanilla
3 eggs
1/2 C. sugar
1/2 C. honey

Preheat oven to 350°F. In a saucepan, cook 1 1/4 cup honey, oil, coffee and vanilla, stirring gently until well blended. Set mixture aside to cool. In a medium bowl, beat eggs and sugar on high speed until thick and pale yellow. Beat the cooled honey mixture into the eggs. Add the Honey Cake Mix and beat until well blended. Scrape batter into a greased 9 x 13 inch pan. Bake for 35 to 40 minutes. As soon as cake is removed from oven use a fork to prick holes all over the surface. Heat 1/2 cup honey and gently pour over the top allowing to seep into cake. Allow cake to cool completely before cutting.

Honey Cake

1 jar Honey Cake Mix
1 1/4 C. honey
3/4 C. vegetable oil
3/4 C. brewed coffee

2 tsp. vanilla
3 eggs
1/2 C. sugar
1/2 C. honey

Preheat oven to 350°F. In a saucepan, cook 1 1/4 cup honey, oil, coffee and vanilla, stirring gently until well blended. Set mixture aside to cool. In a medium bowl, beat eggs and sugar on high speed until thick and pale yellow. Beat the cooled honey mixture into the eggs. Add the Honey Cake Mix and beat until well blended. Scrape batter into a greased 9 x 13 inch pan. Bake for 35 to 40 minutes. As soon as cake is removed from oven use a fork to prick holes all over the surface. Heat 1/2 cup honey and gently pour over the top allowing to seep into cake. Allow cake to cool completely before cutting.

Honey Cake

1 jar Honey Cake Mix
1 1/4 C. honey
3/4 C. vegetable oil
3/4 C. brewed coffee

2 tsp. vanilla
3 eggs
1/2 C. sugar
1/2 C. honey

Preheat oven to 350°F. In a saucepan, cook 1 1/4 cup honey, oil, coffee and vanilla, stirring gently until well blended. Set mixture aside to cool. In a medium bowl, beat eggs and sugar on high speed until thick and pale yellow. Beat the cooled honey mixture into the eggs. Add the Honey Cake Mix and beat until well blended. Scrape batter into a greased 9 x 13 inch pan. Bake for 35 to 40 minutes. As soon as cake is removed from oven use a fork to prick holes all over the surface. Heat 1/2 cup honey and gently pour over the top allowing to seep into cake. Allow cake to cool completely before cutting.

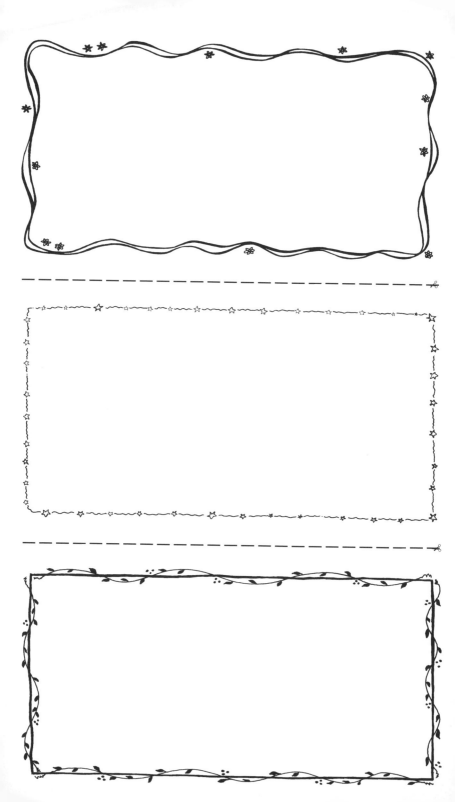

Rhubarb Crunch Mix

3/4 C. quick oats
1 C. brown sugar
1 tsp. cinnamon
1 1/4 C. flour

Sugar Packet:
1 C. sugar
2 T. cornstarch

Layer the ingredients in the order given into a wide-mouth 1-quart canning jar. Pack each layer into place before adding the next ingredient.

Attach a gift tag with the mixing and baking instructions.

Rhubarb Crunch

1 jar Rhubarb Crunch Mix
2/3 C. melted butter or
   margarine
4 C. diced rhubarb
1 tsp. vanilla

Preheat oven to 350°F. Remove sugar packet from jar and place remaining Rhubarb Crunch Mix in a mixing bowl. Add butter, mixing with a spatula until combined and slightly crumbly. Press half of the crumb mixture into the bottom of a greased 7 x 11 inch pan or a 9 inch round pan. Cover with diced rhubarb. In a saucepan, combine sugar packet with 1 C. water and vanilla. Cook, stirring until thick and clear. Pour over rhubarb and top with remaining crumb mixture. Bake for 1 hour.

Rhubarb Crunch

1 jar Rhubarb Crunch Mix
2/3 C. melted butter or
   margarine

4 C. diced rhubarb
1 tsp. vanilla

Preheat oven to 350°F. Remove sugar packet from jar and place remaining Rhubarb Crunch Mix in a mixing bowl. Add butter, mixing with a spatula until combined and slightly crumbly. Press half of the crumb mixture into the bottom of a greased 7 x 11 inch pan or a 9 inch round pan. Cover with diced rhubarb. In a saucepan, combine sugar packet with 1 C. water and vanilla. Cook, stirring until thick and clear. Pour over rhubarb and top with remaining crumb mixture. Bake for 1 hour.

Rhubarb Crunch

1 jar Rhubarb Crunch Mix
2/3 C. melted butter or
   margarine

4 C. diced rhubarb
1 tsp. vanilla

Preheat oven to 350°F. Remove sugar packet from jar and place remaining Rhubarb Crunch Mix in a mixing bowl. Add butter, mixing with a spatula until combined and slightly crumbly. Press half of the crumb mixture into the bottom of a greased 7 x 11 inch pan or a 9 inch round pan. Cover with diced rhubarb. In a saucepan, combine sugar packet with 1 C. water and vanilla. Cook, stirring until thick and clear. Pour over rhubarb and top with remaining crumb mixture. Bake for 1 hour.

Rhubarb Crunch

1 jar Rhubarb Crunch Mix
2/3 C. melted butter or
   margarine

4 C. diced rhubarb
1 tsp. vanilla

Preheat oven to 350°F. Remove sugar packet from jar and place remaining Rhubarb Crunch Mix in a mixing bowl. Add butter, mixing with a spatula until combined and slightly crumbly. Press half of the crumb mixture into the bottom of a greased 7 x 11 inch pan or a 9 inch round pan. Cover with diced rhubarb. In a saucepan, combine sugar packet with 1 C. water and vanilla. Cook, stirring until thick and clear. Pour over rhubarb and top with remaining crumb mixture. Bake for 1 hour.

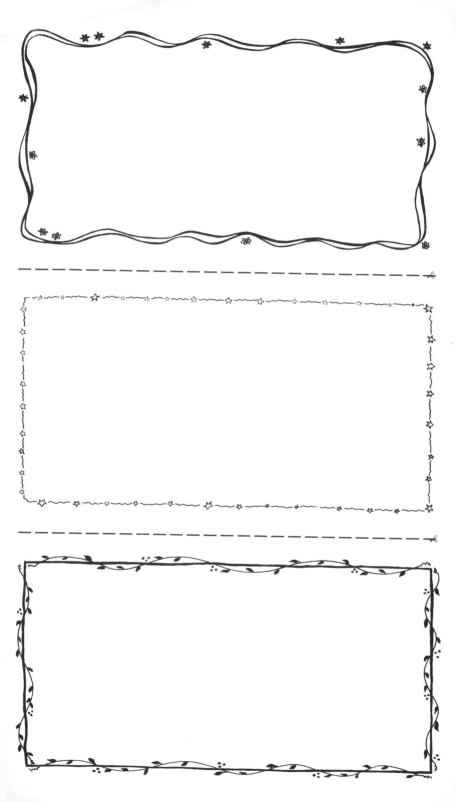

Rhubarb Crunch

1 jar Rhubarb Crunch Mix
2/3 C. melted butter or
  margarine

4 C. diced rhubarb
1 tsp. vanilla

Preheat oven to 350°F. Remove sugar packet from jar and place remaining Rhubarb Crunch Mix in a mixing bowl. Add butter, mixing with a spatula until combined and slightly crumbly. Press half of the crumb mixture into the bottom of a greased 7 x 11 inch pan or a 9 inch round pan. Cover with diced rhubarb. In a saucepan, combine sugar packet with 1 C. water and vanilla. Cook, stirring until thick and clear. Pour over rhubarb and top with remaining crumb mixture. Bake for 1 hour.

Rhubarb Crunch

1 jar Rhubarb Crunch Mix
2/3 C. melted butter or
  margarine

4 C. diced rhubarb
1 tsp. vanilla

Preheat oven to 350°F. Remove sugar packet from jar and place remaining Rhubarb Crunch Mix in a mixing bowl. Add butter, mixing with a spatula until combined and slightly crumbly. Press half of the crumb mixture into the bottom of a greased 7 x 11 inch pan or a 9 inch round pan. Cover with diced rhubarb. In a saucepan, combine sugar packet with 1 C. water and vanilla. Cook, stirring until thick and clear. Pour over rhubarb and top with remaining crumb mixture. Bake for 1 hour.

Rhubarb Crunch

1 jar Rhubarb Crunch Mix
2/3 C. melted butter or
  margarine

4 C. diced rhubarb
1 tsp. vanilla

Preheat oven to 350°F. Remove sugar packet from jar and place remaining Rhubarb Crunch Mix in a mixing bowl. Add butter, mixing with a spatula until combined and slightly crumbly. Press half of the crumb mixture into the bottom of a greased 7 x 11 inch pan or a 9 inch round pan. Cover with diced rhubarb. In a saucepan, combine sugar packet with 1 C. water and vanilla. Cook, stirring until thick and clear. Pour over rhubarb and top with remaining crumb mixture. Bake for 1 hour.

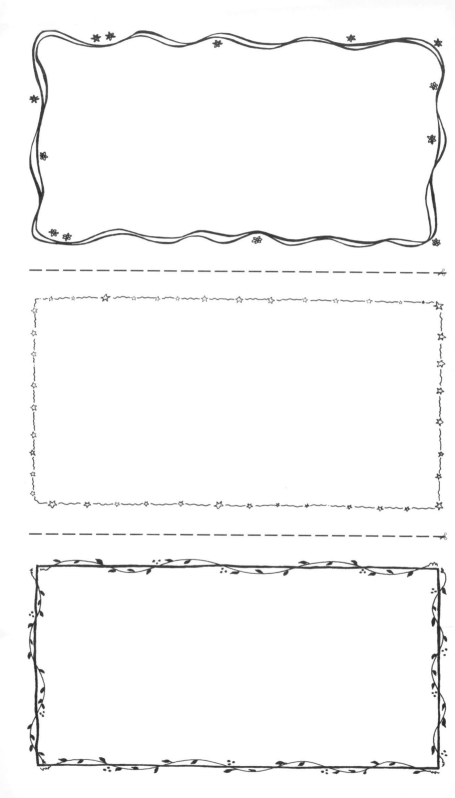

Banana Chocolate Chip Cake Mix

3/4 C. sugar
3/4 C. mini chocolate chips
1/2 C. brown sugar
1 1/4 tsp. baking soda
1 tsp. baking powder
1/2 tsp. salt
1/4 tsp. nutmeg
2 1/4 C. flour

Layer the ingredients in the order given into a wide-mouth 1-quart canning jar. Pack each layer into place before adding the next ingredient.

Attach a gift tag with the mixing and baking instructions.

Banana Chocolate Chip Cake

1 jar Banana Chocolate Chip
   Cake Mix
2 large ripe bananas
3 T. sour cream
2 tsp. vanilla
3 eggs
3/4 C. butter or margarine,
   softened

Preheat oven to 350°F. Combine bananas and sour cream with fork or mixer until evenly blended. Add vanilla and eggs and stir to combine. Empty contents of jar into a mixing bowl, stirring to combine. Add half of the banana mixture and butter. Beat on low speed until dry ingredients are moistened. Beat on medium speed for 1 1/2 minutes then add remaining banana mixture in two parts, beating for 20 to 30 seconds after each addition. Scrape batter into a greased 7 x 11 inch pan. Bake for 35 to 40 minutes. Let cool and dust with powdered sugar to serve.

Banana Chocolate Chip Cake

1 jar Banana Chocolate Chip
  Cake Mix
2 large ripe bananas
3 T. sour cream

2 tsp. vanilla
3 eggs
3/4 C. butter or margarine,
  softened

Preheat oven to 350°F. Combine bananas and sour cream with fork or mixer until evenly blended. Add vanilla and eggs and stir to combine. Empty contents of jar into a mixing bowl, stirring to combine. Add half of the banana mixture and butter. Beat on low speed until dry ingredients are moistened. Beat on medium speed for 1 1/2 minutes then add remaining banana mixture in two parts, beating for 20 to 30 seconds after each addition. Scrape batter into a greased 7 x 11 inch pan. Bake for 35 to 40 minutes. Let cool and dust with powdered sugar to serve.

Banana Chocolate Chip Cake

1 jar Banana Chocolate Chip
  Cake Mix
2 large ripe bananas
3 T. sour cream

2 tsp. vanilla
3 eggs
3/4 C. butter or margarine,
  softened

Preheat oven to 350°F. Combine bananas and sour cream with fork or mixer until evenly blended. Add vanilla and eggs and stir to combine. Empty contents of jar into a mixing bowl, stirring to combine. Add half of the banana mixture and butter. Beat on low speed until dry ingredients are moistened. Beat on medium speed for 1 1/2 minutes then add remaining banana mixture in two parts, beating for 20 to 30 seconds after each addition. Scrape batter into a greased 7 x 11 inch pan. Bake for 35 to 40 minutes. Let cool and dust with powdered sugar to serve.

Banana Chocolate Chip Cake

1 jar Banana Chocolate Chip
  Cake Mix
2 large ripe bananas
3 T. sour cream

2 tsp. vanilla
3 eggs
3/4 C. butter or margarine,
  softened

Preheat oven to 350°F. Combine bananas and sour cream with fork or mixer until evenly blended. Add vanilla and eggs and stir to combine. Empty contents of jar into a mixing bowl, stirring to combine. Add half of the banana mixture and butter. Beat on low speed until dry ingredients are moistened. Beat on medium speed for 1 1/2 minutes then add remaining banana mixture in two parts, beating for 20 to 30 seconds after each addition. Scrape batter into a greased 7 x 11 inch pan. Bake for 35 to 40 minutes. Let cool and dust with powdered sugar to serve.

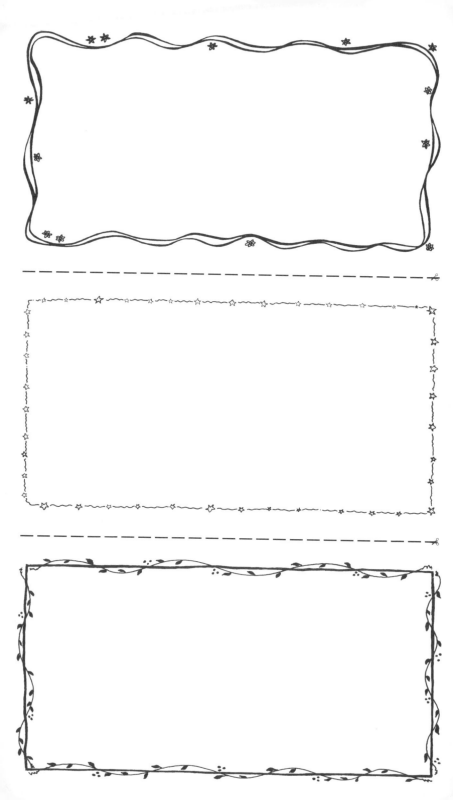

Banana Chocolate Chip Cake

1 jar Banana Chocolate Chip
  Cake Mix
2 large ripe bananas
3 T. sour cream

2 tsp. vanilla
3 eggs
3/4 C. butter or margarine,
  softened

Preheat oven to 350°F. Combine bananas and sour cream with fork or mixer until evenly blended. Add vanilla and eggs and stir to combine. Empty contents of jar into a mixing bowl, stirring to combine. Add half of the banana mixture and butter. Beat on low speed until dry ingredients are moistened. Beat on medium speed for 1 1/2 minutes then add remaining banana mixture in two parts, beating for 20 to 30 seconds after each addition. Scrape batter into a greased 7 x 11 inch pan. Bake for 35 to 40 minutes. Let cool and dust with powdered sugar to serve.

Banana Chocolate Chip Cake

1 jar Banana Chocolate Chip
  Cake Mix
2 large ripe bananas
3 T. sour cream

2 tsp. vanilla
3 eggs
3/4 C. butter or margarine,
  softened

Preheat oven to 350°F. Combine bananas and sour cream with fork or mixer until evenly blended. Add vanilla and eggs and stir to combine. Empty contents of jar into a mixing bowl, stirring to combine. Add half of the banana mixture and butter. Beat on low speed until dry ingredients are moistened. Beat on medium speed for 1 1/2 minutes then add remaining banana mixture in two parts, beating for 20 to 30 seconds after each addition. Scrape batter into a greased 7 x 11 inch pan. Bake for 35 to 40 minutes. Let cool and dust with powdered sugar to serve.

Banana Chocolate Chip Cake

1 jar Banana Chocolate Chip
  Cake Mix
2 large ripe bananas
3 T. sour cream

2 tsp. vanilla
3 eggs
3/4 C. butter or margarine,
  softened

Preheat oven to 350°F. Combine bananas and sour cream with fork or mixer until evenly blended. Add vanilla and eggs and stir to combine. Empty contents of jar into a mixing bowl, stirring to combine. Add half of the banana mixture and butter. Beat on low speed until dry ingredients are moistened. Beat on medium speed for 1 1/2 minutes then add remaining banana mixture in two parts, beating for 20 to 30 seconds after each addition. Scrape batter into a greased 7 x 11 inch pan. Bake for 35 to 40 minutes. Let cool and dust with powdered sugar to serve.

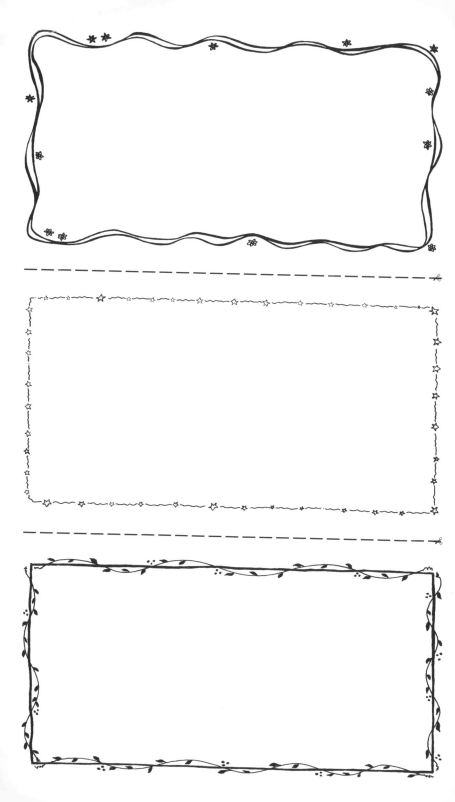

Applesauce Cake Mix

1 C. finely chopped walnuts
1 C. raisins or currants
3/4 tsp. baking soda
1/2 tsp. salt
1 tsp. cinnamon
1/2 tsp. cloves
1/4 tsp. nutmeg
1/4 tsp. allspice
1 1/2 C. flour
3/4 C. brown sugar

Layer the ingredients in the order given into a wide-mouth 1-quart canning jar. Pack each layer into place before adding the next ingredient.

Attach a gift tag with the mixing and baking instructions.

Applesauce Cake

1 jar Applesauce Cake Mix
1/2 C. butter or margarine,
  softened
1 egg
1 C. unsweetened applesauce

Preheat oven to 350°F. Beat butter on high speed until creamy. Scoop 1/2 of the brown sugar from the jar and add to butter. Beat on high speed for 3 to 5 minutes then beat in egg. Add half of the remaining Applesauce Cake Mix and half of the applesauce and beat on low speed until incorporated. Add the remaining Mix and applesauce and continue beating on low speed until completely incorporated. Scrape batter into a greased 9 inch round pan or a greased Bundt pan. Bake for 25 to 30 minutes in the round pan or 50 to 55 in the Bundt pan.

Applesauce Cake

1 jar Applesauce Cake Mix
1/2 C. butter or margarine,
    softened

1 egg
1 C. unsweetened applesauce

Preheat oven to 350°F. Beat butter on high speed until creamy. Scoop 1/2 of the brown sugar from the jar and add to butter. Beat on high speed for 3 to 5 minutes then beat in egg. Add half of the remaining Applesauce Cake Mix and half of the applesauce and beat on low speed until incorporated. Add the remaining Mix and applesauce and continue beating on low speed until completely incorporated. Scrape batter into a greased 9 inch round pan or a greased Bundt pan. Bake for 25 to 30 minutes in the round pan or 50 to 55 in the Bundt pan.

Applesauce Cake

1 jar Applesauce Cake Mix
1/2 C. butter or margarine,
    softened

1 egg
1 C. unsweetened applesauce

Preheat oven to 350°F. Beat butter on high speed until creamy. Scoop 1/2 of the brown sugar from the jar and add to butter. Beat on high speed for 3 to 5 minutes then beat in egg. Add half of the remaining Applesauce Cake Mix and half of the applesauce and beat on low speed until incorporated. Add the remaining Mix and applesauce and continue beating on low speed until completely incorporated. Scrape batter into a greased 9 inch round pan or a greased Bundt pan. Bake for 25 to 30 minutes in the round pan or 50 to 55 in the Bundt pan.

Applesauce Cake

1 jar Applesauce Cake Mix
1/2 C. butter or margarine,
    softened

1 egg
1 C. unsweetened applesauce

Preheat oven to 350°F. Beat butter on high speed until creamy. Scoop 1/2 of the brown sugar from the jar and add to butter. Beat on high speed for 3 to 5 minutes then beat in egg. Add half of the remaining Applesauce Cake Mix and half of the applesauce and beat on low speed until incorporated. Add the remaining Mix and applesauce and continue beating on low speed until completely incorporated. Scrape batter into a greased 9 inch round pan or a greased Bundt pan. Bake for 25 to 30 minutes in the round pan or 50 to 55 in the Bundt pan.

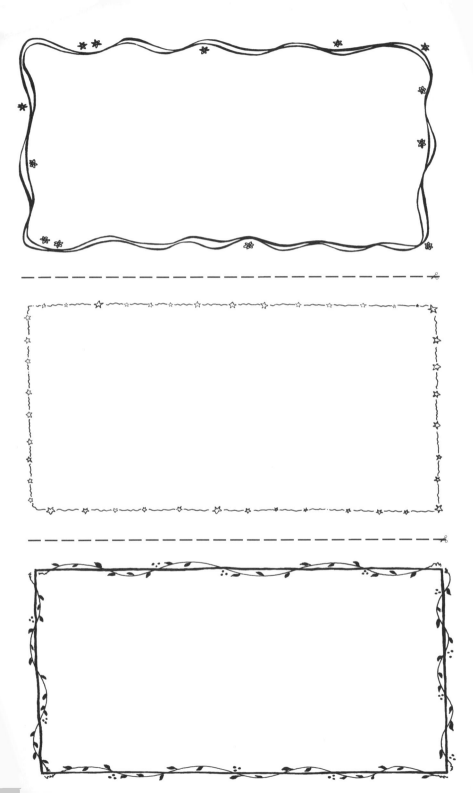

Applesauce Cake

1 jar Applesauce Cake Mix
1/2 C. butter or margarine,
   softened

1 egg
1 C. unsweetened applesauce

Preheat oven to 350°F. Beat butter on high speed until creamy. Scoop 1/2 of the brown sugar from the jar and add to butter. Beat on high speed for 3 to 5 minutes then beat in egg. Add half of the remaining Applesauce Cake Mix and half of the applesauce and beat on low speed until incorporated. Add the remaining Mix and applesauce and continue beating on low speed until completely incorporated. Scrape batter into a greased 9 inch round pan or a greased Bundt pan. Bake for 25 to 30 minutes in the round pan or 50 to 55 in the Bundt pan.

Applesauce Cake

1 jar Applesauce Cake Mix
1/2 C. butter or margarine,
   softened

1 egg
1 C. unsweetened applesauce

Preheat oven to 350°F. Beat butter on high speed until creamy. Scoop 1/2 of the brown sugar from the jar and add to butter. Beat on high speed for 3 to 5 minutes then beat in egg. Add half of the remaining Applesauce Cake Mix and half of the applesauce and beat on low speed until incorporated. Add the remaining Mix and applesauce and continue beating on low speed until completely incorporated. Scrape batter into a greased 9 inch round pan or a greased Bundt pan. Bake for 25 to 30 minutes in the round pan or 50 to 55 in the Bundt pan.

Applesauce Cake

1 jar Applesauce Cake Mix
1/2 C. butter or margarine,
   softened

1 egg
1 C. unsweetened applesauce

Preheat oven to 350°F. Beat butter on high speed until creamy. Scoop 1/2 of the brown sugar from the jar and add to butter. Beat on high speed for 3 to 5 minutes then beat in egg. Add half of the remaining Applesauce Cake Mix and half of the applesauce and beat on low speed until incorporated. Add the remaining Mix and applesauce and continue beating on low speed until completely incorporated. Scrape batter into a greased 9 inch round pan or a greased Bundt pan. Bake for 25 to 30 minutes in the round pan or 50 to 55 in the Bundt pan.

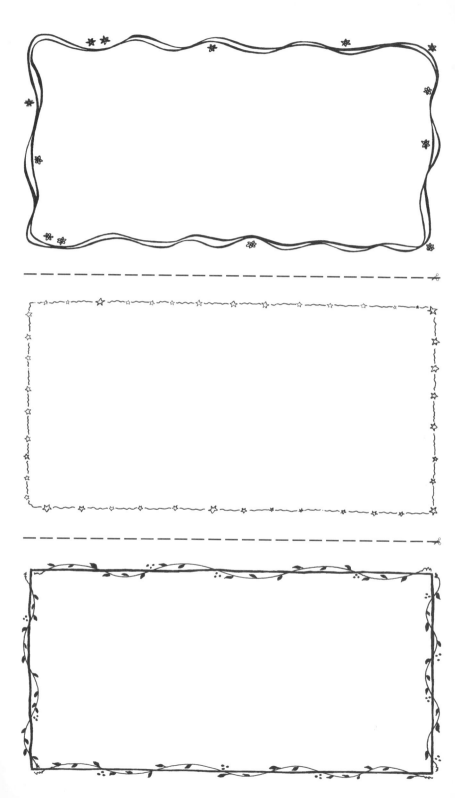

Pumpkin Chocolate Cake Mix

1/2 C. finely chopped pecans
1 C. chocolate chips
1 1/4 C. flour
2 T. unsweetened cocoa
1 1/4 C. sugar
1/2 tsp. salt
1 tsp. baking powder
1/2 tsp. baking soda
1 tsp. cinnamon
1/4 tsp. cloves
1/4 tsp. nutmeg

Layer the ingredients in the order given into a wide-mouth 1-quart canning jar. Pack each layer into place before adding the next ingredient.

Attach a gift tag with the mixing and baking instructions.

❁ A half-yard of fabric should make eight wide-mouth jar covers. ❁

Pumpkin Chocolate Cake

1 jar Pumpkin Chocolate Cake Mix
1/2 C. vegetable oil
2 eggs
1 (15 oz.) can pumpkin

Preheat oven to 350°F. In a medium bowl, whisk together oil and eggs. Blend in pumpkin. Add Pumpkin Chocolate Cake Mix and beat on low speed for 1 minute. Scrape bowl sides and beat for another 2 minutes on medium speed. Scrape batter into a greased 7 x 11 inch pan or 9 x 2 inch round pan. Bake for 25 to 35 minutes.

Pumpkin Chocolate Cake

1 jar Pumpkin Chocolate Cake Mix   2 eggs
1/2 C. vegetable oil   1 (15 oz.) can pumpkin

     Preheat oven to 350°F. In a medium bowl, whisk together oil and eggs. Blend in pumpkin. Add Pumpkin Chocolate Cake Mix and beat on low speed for 1 minute. Scrape bowl sides and beat for another 2 minutes on medium speed. Scrape batter into a greased 7 x 11 inch pan or 9 x 2 inch round pan. Bake for 25 to 35 minutes.

Pumpkin Chocolate Cake

1 jar Pumpkin Chocolate Cake Mix   2 eggs
1/2 C. vegetable oil   1 (15 oz.) can pumpkin

     Preheat oven to 350°F. In a medium bowl, whisk together oil and eggs. Blend in pumpkin. Add Pumpkin Chocolate Cake Mix and beat on low speed for 1 minute. Scrape bowl sides and beat for another 2 minutes on medium speed. Scrape batter into a greased 7 x 11 inch pan or 9 x 2 inch round pan. Bake for 25 to 35 minutes.

Pumpkin Chocolate Cake

1 jar Pumpkin Chocolate Cake Mix   2 eggs
1/2 C. vegetable oil   1 (15 oz.) can pumpkin

     Preheat oven to 350°F. In a medium bowl, whisk together oil and eggs. Blend in pumpkin. Add Pumpkin Chocolate Cake Mix and beat on low speed for 1 minute. Scrape bowl sides and beat for another 2 minutes on medium speed. Scrape batter into a greased 7 x 11 inch pan or 9 x 2 inch round pan. Bake for 25 to 35 minutes.

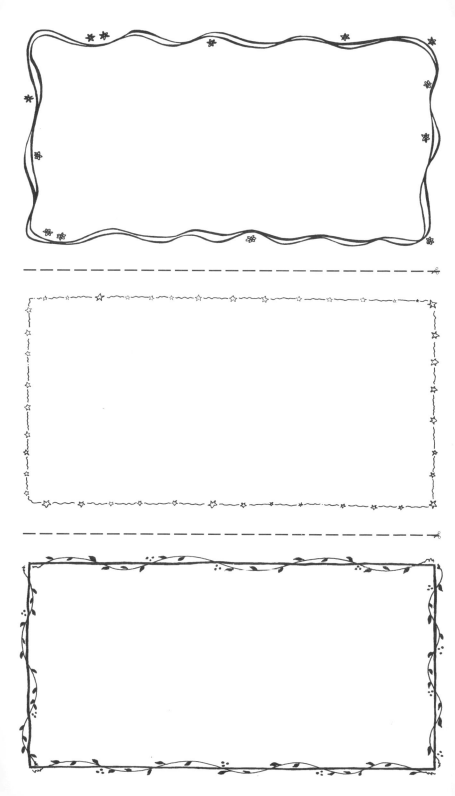

Pumpkin Chocolate Cake

1 jar Pumpkin Chocolate Cake Mix   2 eggs
1/2 C. vegetable oil   1 (15 oz.) can pumpkin

Preheat oven to 350°F. In a medium bowl, whisk together oil and eggs. Blend in pumpkin. Add Pumpkin Chocolate Cake Mix and beat on low speed for 1 minute. Scrape bowl sides and beat for another 2 minutes on medium speed. Scrape batter into a greased 7 x 11 inch pan or 9 x 2 inch round pan. Bake for 25 to 35 minutes.

Pumpkin Chocolate Cake

1 jar Pumpkin Chocolate Cake Mix   2 eggs
1/2 C. vegetable oil   1 (15 oz.) can pumpkin

Preheat oven to 350°F. In a medium bowl, whisk together oil and eggs. Blend in pumpkin. Add Pumpkin Chocolate Cake Mix and beat on low speed for 1 minute. Scrape bowl sides and beat for another 2 minutes on medium speed. Scrape batter into a greased 7 x 11 inch pan or 9 x 2 inch round pan. Bake for 25 to 35 minutes.

Pumpkin Chocolate Cake

1 jar Pumpkin Chocolate Cake Mix   2 eggs
1/2 C. vegetable oil   1 (15 oz.) can pumpkin

Preheat oven to 350°F. In a medium bowl, whisk together oil and eggs. Blend in pumpkin. Add Pumpkin Chocolate Cake Mix and beat on low speed for 1 minute. Scrape bowl sides and beat for another 2 minutes on medium speed. Scrape batter into a greased 7 x 11 inch pan or 9 x 2 inch round pan. Bake for 25 to 35 minutes.

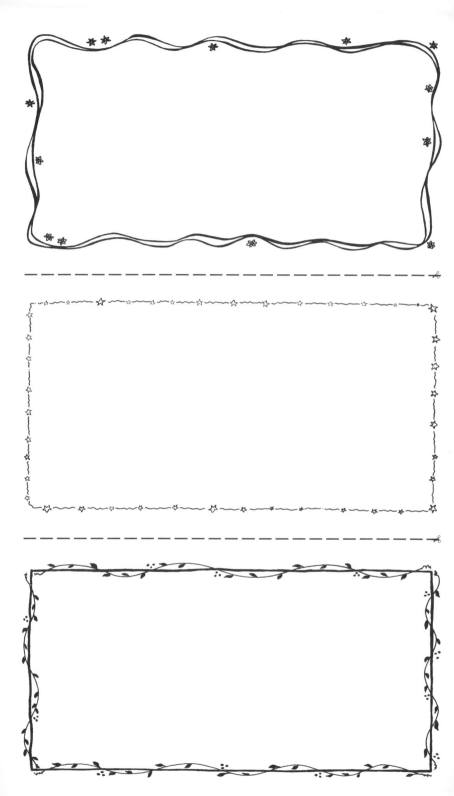

Chocolate Bundt Cake Mix

1 C. sugar
1 (3.4 oz.) pkg. chocolate pudding
1 1/2 C. flour
2 tsp. baking powder
1 tsp. salt
1/2 C. finely chopped walnuts
1 C. mini chocolate chips

Layer the ingredients in the order given into a wide-mouth 1-quart canning jar. Pack each layer into place before adding the next ingredient.

Attach a gift tag with the mixing and baking instructions.

Chocolate Bundt Cake

1 jar Chocolate Bundt Cake Mix
2 eggs
1/2 C. vegetable oil
1/2 C. sour cream
1/2 C. milk
1/2 C. melted chocolate frosting

Preheat oven to 350°F. Empty contents of jar into a large mixing bowl, stirring to combine. Make a well in the center and add eggs, oil, sour cream and milk. Beat on medium speed for 2 minutes. Transfer to a greased Bundt pan and bake for 45 to 55 minutes. Allow to cool completely before inverting onto a serving plate. Drizzle melted chocolate frosting over the top.

Chocolate Bundt Cake

1 jar Chocolate Bundt Cake Mix
2 eggs
1/2 C. vegetable oil

1/2 C. sour cream
1/2 C. milk
1/2 C. melted chocolate frosting

Preheat oven to 350°F. Empty contents of jar into a large mixing bowl, stirring to combine. Make a well in the center and add eggs, oil, sour cream and milk. Beat on medium speed for 2 minutes. Transfer to a greased Bundt pan and bake for 45 to 55 minutes. Allow to cool completely before inverting onto a serving plate. Drizzle melted chocolate frosting over the top.

Chocolate Bundt Cake

1 jar Chocolate Bundt Cake Mix
2 eggs
1/2 C. vegetable oil

1/2 C. sour cream
1/2 C. milk
1/2 C. melted chocolate frosting

Preheat oven to 350°F. Empty contents of jar into a large mixing bowl, stirring to combine. Make a well in the center and add eggs, oil, sour cream and milk. Beat on medium speed for 2 minutes. Transfer to a greased Bundt pan and bake for 45 to 55 minutes. Allow to cool completely before inverting onto a serving plate. Drizzle melted chocolate frosting over the top.

Chocolate Bundt Cake

1 jar Chocolate Bundt Cake Mix
2 eggs
1/2 C. vegetable oil

1/2 C. sour cream
1/2 C. milk
1/2 C. melted chocolate frosting

Preheat oven to 350°F. Empty contents of jar into a large mixing bowl, stirring to combine. Make a well in the center and add eggs, oil, sour cream and milk. Beat on medium speed for 2 minutes. Transfer to a greased Bundt pan and bake for 45 to 55 minutes. Allow to cool completely before inverting onto a serving plate. Drizzle melted chocolate frosting over the top.

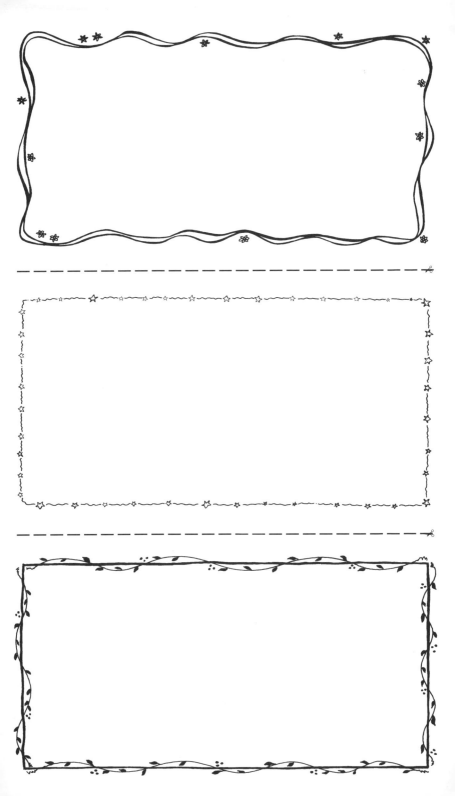

Chocolate Bundt Cake

1 jar Chocolate Bundt Cake Mix
2 eggs
1/2 C. vegetable oil

1/2 C. sour cream
1/2 C. milk
1/2 C. melted chocolate frosting

Preheat oven to 350°F. Empty contents of jar into a large mixing bowl, stirring to combine. Make a well in the center and add eggs, oil, sour cream and milk. Beat on medium speed for 2 minutes. Transfer to a greased Bundt pan and bake for 45 to 55 minutes. Allow to cool completely before inverting onto a serving plate. Drizzle melted chocolate frosting over the top.

Chocolate Bundt Cake

1 jar Chocolate Bundt Cake Mix
2 eggs
1/2 C. vegetable oil

1/2 C. sour cream
1/2 C. milk
1/2 C. melted chocolate frosting

Preheat oven to 350°F. Empty contents of jar into a large mixing bowl, stirring to combine. Make a well in the center and add eggs, oil, sour cream and milk. Beat on medium speed for 2 minutes. Transfer to a greased Bundt pan and bake for 45 to 55 minutes. Allow to cool completely before inverting onto a serving plate. Drizzle melted chocolate frosting over the top.

Chocolate Bundt Cake

1 jar Chocolate Bundt Cake Mix
2 eggs
1/2 C. vegetable oil

1/2 C. sour cream
1/2 C. milk
1/2 C. melted chocolate frosting

Preheat oven to 350°F. Empty contents of jar into a large mixing bowl, stirring to combine. Make a well in the center and add eggs, oil, sour cream and milk. Beat on medium speed for 2 minutes. Transfer to a greased Bundt pan and bake for 45 to 55 minutes. Allow to cool completely before inverting onto a serving plate. Drizzle melted chocolate frosting over the top.

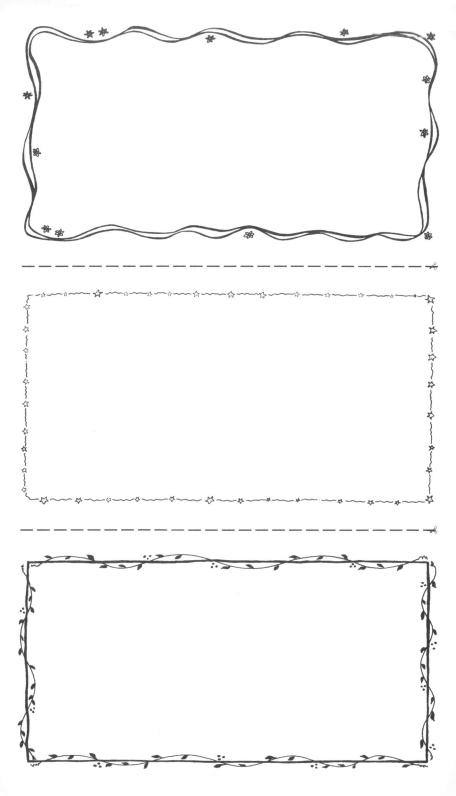

Blueberry Cobbler Mix

2/3 C. sugar
3/4 C. yellow cornmeal
1 T. baking powder
1 1/2 tsp. salt
2 2/3 C. flour

Layer the ingredients in the order given into a wide-mouth 1-quart canning jar. Pack each layer into place before adding the next ingredient.

Attach a gift tag with the mixing and baking instructions.

Blueberry Cobbler

1 jar Blueberry Cobbler Mix
4 pints fresh or frozen
   blueberries
1 C. sugar
1/4 C. cornstarch
2 tsp. lemon zest
3/4 C. butter or margarine,
   cold
1 1/4 C. whole milk or cream

Preheat oven to 375°F. In a mixing bowl, combine blueberries, sugar, cornstarch and lemon zest. Transfer blueberry mixture to a greased 7 x 11 inch pan. In another bowl, cut butter into Blueberry Cobbler Mix. Make a well in the center and pour in milk. Stir until combined then knead dough against the sides of the bowl by hand 5 to 10 times. Transfer to a floured surface and roll to 1/4 to 1/2 inch thickness. Cut dough into circles or squares and place over blueberry mixture. Bake for 50 to 55 minutes.

Blueberry Cobbler

1 jar Blueberry Cobbler Mix
4 pints fresh or frozen
   blueberries
1 C. sugar

1/4 C. cornstarch
2 tsp. lemon zest
3/4 C. butter or margarine, cold
1 1/4 C. whole milk or cream

Preheat oven to 375°F. In a mixing bowl, combine blueberries, sugar, cornstarch and lemon zest. Transfer blueberry mixture to a greased 7 x 11 inch pan. In another bowl, cut butter into Blueberry Cobbler Mix. Make a well in the center and pour in milk. Stir until combined then knead dough against the sides of the bowl by hand 5 to 10 times. Transfer to a floured surface and roll to 1/4 to 1/2 inch thickness. Cut dough into circles or squares and place over blueberry mixture. Bake for 50 to 55 minutes.

Blueberry Cobbler

1 jar Blueberry Cobbler Mix
4 pints fresh or frozen
   blueberries
1 C. sugar

1/4 C. cornstarch
2 tsp. lemon zest
3/4 C. butter or margarine, cold
1 1/4 C. whole milk or cream

Preheat oven to 375°F. In a mixing bowl, combine blueberries, sugar, cornstarch and lemon zest. Transfer blueberry mixture to a greased 7 x 11 inch pan. In another bowl, cut butter into Blueberry Cobbler Mix. Make a well in the center and pour in milk. Stir until combined then knead dough against the sides of the bowl by hand 5 to 10 times. Transfer to a floured surface and roll to 1/4 to 1/2 inch thickness. Cut dough into circles or squares and place over blueberry mixture. Bake for 50 to 55 minutes.

Blueberry Cobbler

1 jar Blueberry Cobbler Mix
4 pints fresh or frozen
   blueberries
1 C. sugar

1/4 C. cornstarch
2 tsp. lemon zest
3/4 C. butter or margarine, cold
1 1/4 C. whole milk or cream

Preheat oven to 375°F. In a mixing bowl, combine blueberries, sugar, cornstarch and lemon zest. Transfer blueberry mixture to a greased 7 x 11 inch pan. In another bowl, cut butter into Blueberry Cobbler Mix. Make a well in the center and pour in milk. Stir until combined then knead dough against the sides of the bowl by hand 5 to 10 times. Transfer to a floured surface and roll to 1/4 to 1/2 inch thickness. Cut dough into circles or squares and place over blueberry mixture. Bake for 50 to 55 minutes.

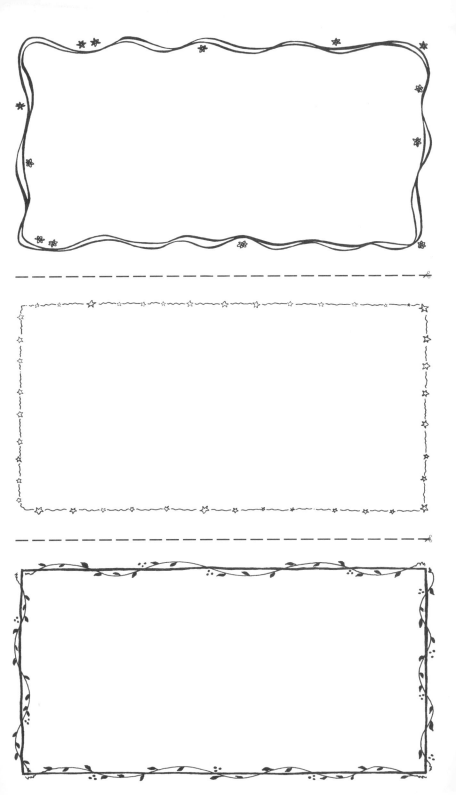

Blueberry Cobbler

1 jar Blueberry Cobbler Mix	1/4 C. cornstarch
4 pints fresh or frozen blueberries	2 tsp. lemon zest
	3/4 C. butter or margarine, cold
1 C. sugar	1 1/4 C. whole milk or cream

Preheat oven to 375°F. In a mixing bowl, combine blueberries, sugar, cornstarch and lemon zest. Transfer blueberry mixture to a greased 7 x 11 inch pan. In another bowl, cut butter into Blueberry Cobbler Mix. Make a well in the center and pour in milk. Stir until combined then knead dough against the sides of the bowl by hand 5 to 10 times. Transfer to a floured surface and roll to 1/4 to 1/2 inch thickness. Cut dough into circles or squares and place over blueberry mixture. Bake for 50 to 55 minutes.

Blueberry Cobbler

1 jar Blueberry Cobbler Mix	1/4 C. cornstarch
4 pints fresh or frozen blueberries	2 tsp. lemon zest
	3/4 C. butter or margarine, cold
1 C. sugar	1 1/4 C. whole milk or cream

Preheat oven to 375°F. In a mixing bowl, combine blueberries, sugar, cornstarch and lemon zest. Transfer blueberry mixture to a greased 7 x 11 inch pan. In another bowl, cut butter into Blueberry Cobbler Mix. Make a well in the center and pour in milk. Stir until combined then knead dough against the sides of the bowl by hand 5 to 10 times. Transfer to a floured surface and roll to 1/4 to 1/2 inch thickness. Cut dough into circles or squares and place over blueberry mixture. Bake for 50 to 55 minutes.

Blueberry Cobbler

1 jar Blueberry Cobbler Mix	1/4 C. cornstarch
4 pints fresh or frozen blueberries	2 tsp. lemon zest
	3/4 C. butter or margarine, cold
1 C. sugar	1 1/4 C. whole milk or cream

Preheat oven to 375°F. In a mixing bowl, combine blueberries, sugar, cornstarch and lemon zest. Transfer blueberry mixture to a greased 7 x 11 inch pan. In another bowl, cut butter into Blueberry Cobbler Mix. Make a well in the center and pour in milk. Stir until combined then knead dough against the sides of the bowl by hand 5 to 10 times. Transfer to a floured surface and roll to 1/4 to 1/2 inch thickness. Cut dough into circles or squares and place over blueberry mixture. Bake for 50 to 55 minutes.

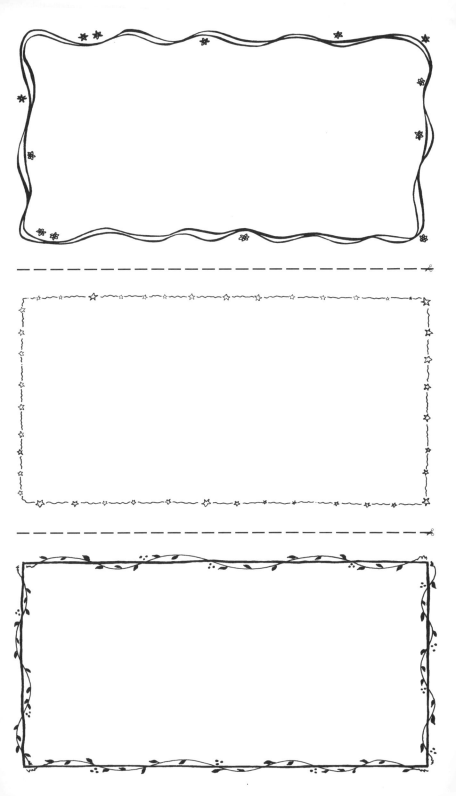

Apple Pandowdy Mix

2 T. sugar
1 tsp. salt
2 3/4 C. flour

Seasoning Packet:

1/2 C. flour
1 tsp. cinnamon
1/2 tsp. nutmeg
1/2 tsp. salt
1/2 C. brown sugar

Layer the ingredients in the order given into a wide-mouth 1-quart canning jar. Pack each layer into place before adding the next ingredient. Mix and place the seasonings in a small plastic bag. Place the packet on top of the flour.

Attach a gift tag with the mixing and baking instructions.

Apple Pandowdy

1 jar Apple Pandowdy Mix
1 C. plus 2 T. shortening
6 tart apples, peeled & sliced
1/4 C. butter or margarine,
    softened

Preheat oven to 400°F. Remove seasoning packet from jar and empty remaining jar contents into a mixing bowl, stirring to combine. Cut in shortening until mixture resembles fine crumbs. Make a well in the center and drizzle 1/3 C. plus 2 T. ice water over the top. Using a spatula side, cut to combine ice water and crumb mixture. Knead dough 3 to 4 times against the side of the bowl until all dry ingredients are incorporated. Transfer to a floured surface and roll to 1/8" thickness. Refrigerate dough while preparing filling. Toss apple slices with seasoning packet and place in a greased 9 x 13 inch pan. Dot with butter. Cover with rolled dough and make knife slits in top so steam can escape and syrup bubble up. Bake at 400° until top has browned, roughly 30 minutes. Reduce temperature to 350° and bake another 30 minutes.

Apple Pandowdy

1 jar Apple Pandowdy Mix   6 tart apples, peeled & sliced
1 C. plus 2 T. shortening   1/4 C. butter or margarine, softened

Preheat oven to 400°F. Remove seasoning packet from jar and empty remaining jar contents into a mixing bowl, stirring to combine. Cut in shortening until mixture resembles fine crumbs. Make a well in the center and drizzle 1/3 C. plus 2 T. ice water over the top. Using a spatula side, cut to combine ice water and crumb mixture. Knead dough 3 to 4 times against the side of the bowl until all dry ingredients are incorporated. Transfer to a floured surface and roll to 1/8" thickness. Refrigerate dough while preparing filling. Toss apple slices with seasoning packet and place in a greased 9 x 13 inch pan. Dot with butter. Cover with rolled dough and make knife slits in top so steam can escape and syrup bubble up. Bake at 400° until top has browned, roughly 30 minutes. Reduce temperature to 350° and bake another 30 minutes.

Apple Pandowdy

1 jar Apple Pandowdy Mix   6 tart apples, peeled & sliced
1 C. plus 2 T. shortening   1/4 C. butter or margarine, softened

Preheat oven to 400°F. Remove seasoning packet from jar and empty remaining jar contents into a mixing bowl, stirring to combine. Cut in shortening until mixture resembles fine crumbs. Make a well in the center and drizzle 1/3 C. plus 2 T. ice water over the top. Using a spatula side, cut to combine ice water and crumb mixture. Knead dough 3 to 4 times against the side of the bowl until all dry ingredients are incorporated. Transfer to a floured surface and roll to 1/8" thickness. Refrigerate dough while preparing filling. Toss apple slices with seasoning packet and place in a greased 9 x 13 inch pan. Dot with butter. Cover with rolled dough and make knife slits in top so steam can escape and syrup bubble up. Bake at 400° until top has browned, roughly 30 minutes. Reduce temperature to 350° and bake another 30 minutes.

Apple Pandowdy

1 jar Apple Pandowdy Mix   6 tart apples, peeled & sliced
1 C. plus 2 T. shortening   1/4 C. butter or margarine, softened

Preheat oven to 400°F. Remove seasoning packet from jar and empty remaining jar contents into a mixing bowl, stirring to combine. Cut in shortening until mixture resembles fine crumbs. Make a well in the center and drizzle 1/3 C. plus 2 T. ice water over the top. Using a spatula side, cut to combine ice water and crumb mixture. Knead dough 3 to 4 times against the side of the bowl until all dry ingredients are incorporated. Transfer to a floured surface and roll to 1/8" thickness. Refrigerate dough while preparing filling. Toss apple slices with seasoning packet and place in a greased 9 x 13 inch pan. Dot with butter. Cover with rolled dough and make knife slits in top so steam can escape and syrup bubble up. Bake at 400° until top has browned, roughly 30 minutes. Reduce temperature to 350° and bake another 30 minutes.

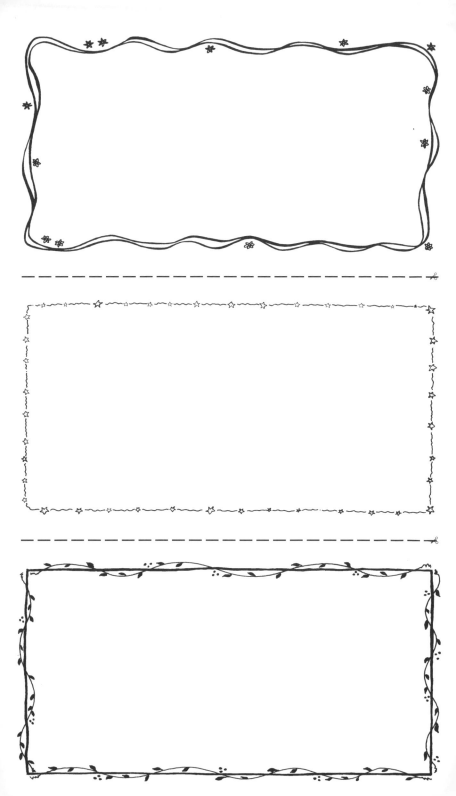

Apple Pandowdy

1 jar Apple Pandowdy Mix
1 C. plus 2 T. shortening

6 tart apples, peeled & sliced
1/4 C. butter or margarine, softened

Preheat oven to 400°F. Remove seasoning packet from jar and empty remaining jar contents into a mixing bowl, stirring to combine. Cut in shortening until mixture resembles fine crumbs. Make a well in the center and drizzle 1/3 C. plus 2 T. ice water over the top. Using a spatula side, cut to combine ice water and crumb mixture. Knead dough 3 to 4 times against the side of the bowl until all dry ingredients are incorporated. Transfer to a floured surface and roll to 1/8" thickness. Refrigerate dough while preparing filling. Toss apple slices with seasoning packet and place in a greased 9 x 13 inch pan. Dot with butter. Cover with rolled dough and make knife slits in top so steam can escape and syrup bubble up. Bake at 400° until top has browned, roughly 30 minutes. Reduce temperature to 350° and bake another 30 minutes.

Apple Pandowdy

1 jar Apple Pandowdy Mix
1 C. plus 2 T. shortening

6 tart apples, peeled & sliced
1/4 C. butter or margarine, softened

Preheat oven to 400°F. Remove seasoning packet from jar and empty remaining jar contents into a mixing bowl, stirring to combine. Cut in shortening until mixture resembles fine crumbs. Make a well in the center and drizzle 1/3 C. plus 2 T. ice water over the top. Using a spatula side, cut to combine ice water and crumb mixture. Knead dough 3 to 4 times against the side of the bowl until all dry ingredients are incorporated. Transfer to a floured surface and roll to 1/8" thickness. Refrigerate dough while preparing filling. Toss apple slices with seasoning packet and place in a greased 9 x 13 inch pan. Dot with butter. Cover with rolled dough and make knife slits in top so steam can escape and syrup bubble up. Bake at 400° until top has browned, roughly 30 minutes. Reduce temperature to 350° and bake another 30 minutes.

Apple Pandowdy

1 jar Apple Pandowdy Mix
1 C. plus 2 T. shortening

6 tart apples, peeled & sliced
1/4 C. butter or margarine, softened

Preheat oven to 400°F. Remove seasoning packet from jar and empty remaining jar contents into a mixing bowl, stirring to combine. Cut in shortening until mixture resembles fine crumbs. Make a well in the center and drizzle 1/3 C. plus 2 T. ice water over the top. Using a spatula side, cut to combine ice water and crumb mixture. Knead dough 3 to 4 times against the side of the bowl until all dry ingredients are incorporated. Transfer to a floured surface and roll to 1/8" thickness. Refrigerate dough while preparing filling. Toss apple slices with seasoning packet and place in a greased 9 x 13 inch pan. Dot with butter. Cover with rolled dough and make knife slits in top so steam can escape and syrup bubble up. Bake at 400° until top has browned, roughly 30 minutes. Reduce temperature to 350° and bake another 30 minutes.

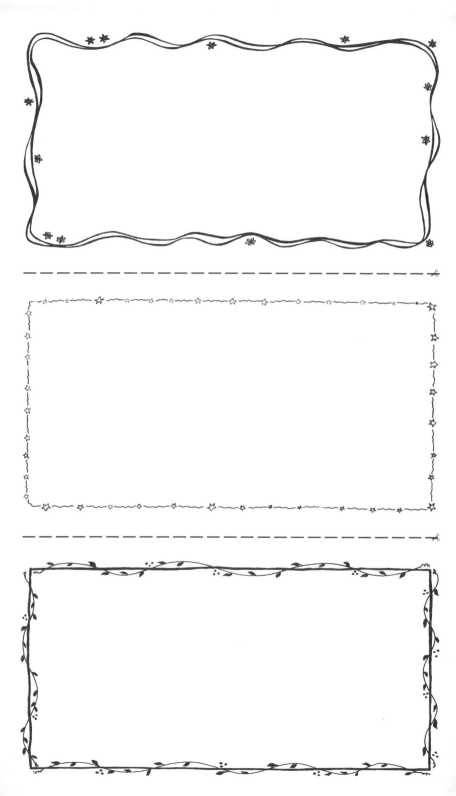

Cherry Crumb Cake Mix

1 1/3 C. sugar
3/4 C. quick oats
1 T. baking powder
1 tsp. salt
2 C. flour

Layer the ingredients in the order given into a wide-mouth 1-quart canning jar. Pack each layer into place before adding the next ingredient.

Attach a gift tag with the mixing and baking instructions.

Cherry Crumb Cake

1 jar Cherry Crumb Cake Mix
3/4 C. butter or margarine,
  cold
2 eggs
1 (25 oz.) can cherry pie filling

Preheat oven to 350°F. Empty contents of jar into a mixing bowl, stirring to combine. Cut butter into dry mixture until fine and crumbly. Add eggs and mix with a fork until combined but still crumbly in texture. Press half of the crumb mixture into a greased 9 x 13 inch pan. Top with cherry pie filling. Sprinkle remaining crumb mixture on top. Bake for 35 to 40 minutes.

Cherry Crumb Cake

1 jar Cherry Crumb Cake Mix   2 eggs
3/4 C. butter or margarine, cold 1 (25 oz.) can cherry pie filling

Preheat oven to 350°F. Empty contents of jar into a mixing bowl, stirring to combine. Cut butter into dry mixture until fine and crumbly. Add eggs and mix with a fork until combined but still crumbly in texture. Press half of the crumb mixture into a greased 9 x 13 inch pan. Top with cherry pie filling. Sprinkle remaining crumb mixture on top. Bake for 35 to 40 minutes.

Cherry Crumb Cake

1 jar Cherry Crumb Cake Mix   2 eggs
3/4 C. butter or margarine, cold 1 (25 oz.) can cherry pie filling

Preheat oven to 350°F. Empty contents of jar into a mixing bowl, stirring to combine. Cut butter into dry mixture until fine and crumbly. Add eggs and mix with a fork until combined but still crumbly in texture. Press half of the crumb mixture into a greased 9 x 13 inch pan. Top with cherry pie filling. Sprinkle remaining crumb mixture on top. Bake for 35 to 40 minutes.

Cherry Crumb Cake

1 jar Cherry Crumb Cake Mix   2 eggs
3/4 C. butter or margarine, cold 1 (25 oz.) can cherry pie filling

Preheat oven to 350°F. Empty contents of jar into a mixing bowl, stirring to combine. Cut butter into dry mixture until fine and crumbly. Add eggs and mix with a fork until combined but still crumbly in texture. Press half of the crumb mixture into a greased 9 x 13 inch pan. Top with cherry pie filling. Sprinkle remaining crumb mixture on top. Bake for 35 to 40 minutes.

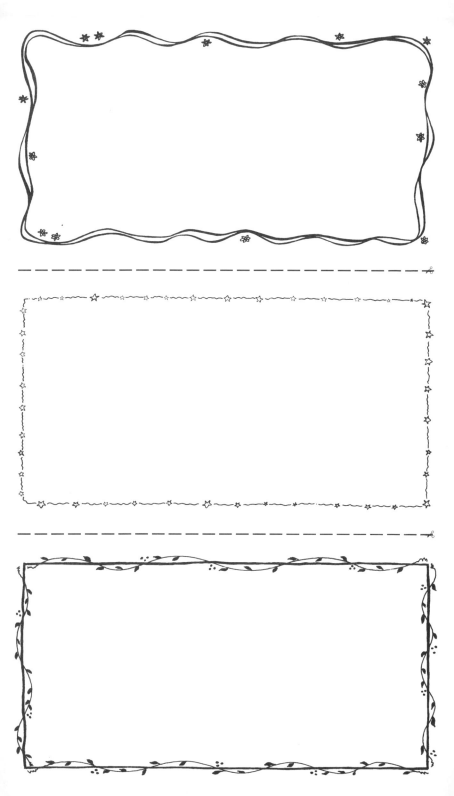

Cherry Crumb Cake

1 jar Cherry Crumb Cake Mix   2 eggs
3/4 C. butter or margarine, cold   1 (25 oz.) can cherry pie filling

Preheat oven to 350°F. Empty contents of jar into a mixing bowl, stirring to combine. Cut butter into dry mixture until fine and crumbly. Add eggs and mix with a fork until combined but still crumbly in texture. Press half of the crumb mixture into a greased 9 x 13 inch pan. Top with cherry pie filling. Sprinkle remaining crumb mixture on top. Bake for 35 to 40 minutes.

Cherry Crumb Cake

1 jar Cherry Crumb Cake Mix   2 eggs
3/4 C. butter or margarine, cold   1 (25 oz.) can cherry pie filling

Preheat oven to 350°F. Empty contents of jar into a mixing bowl, stirring to combine. Cut butter into dry mixture until fine and crumbly. Add eggs and mix with a fork until combined but still crumbly in texture. Press half of the crumb mixture into a greased 9 x 13 inch pan. Top with cherry pie filling. Sprinkle remaining crumb mixture on top. Bake for 35 to 40 minutes.

Cherry Crumb Cake

1 jar Cherry Crumb Cake Mix   2 eggs
3/4 C. butter or margarine, cold   1 (25 oz.) can cherry pie filling

Preheat oven to 350°F. Empty contents of jar into a mixing bowl, stirring to combine. Cut butter into dry mixture until fine and crumbly. Add eggs and mix with a fork until combined but still crumbly in texture. Press half of the crumb mixture into a greased 9 x 13 inch pan. Top with cherry pie filling. Sprinkle remaining crumb mixture on top. Bake for 35 to 40 minutes.

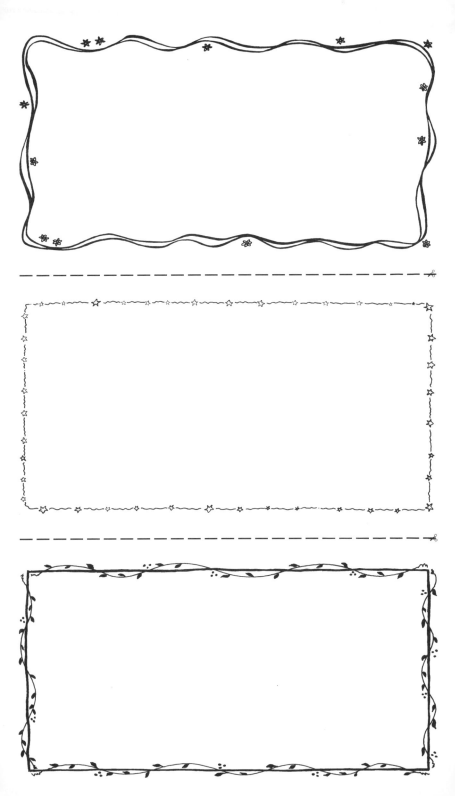

Black Walnut Cake Mix

1 C. finely chopped black walnuts
2 1/4 C. flour
1 T. baking powder
1/2 tsp. salt
1 C. sugar

Layer the ingredients in the order given into a wide-mouth 1-quart canning jar. Pack each layer into place before adding the next ingredient.

Attach a gift tag with the mixing and baking instructions.

❀ For a different look, place a small amount of stuffing under a fabric cover before attaching to "puff" the top. ❀

Black Walnut Cake

1 jar Black Walnut Cake Mix
3/4 C. shortening
3 egg yolks
1 tsp. vanilla
1/2 tsp. almond extract
1 C. whole milk
3 egg whites
1/4 C. sugar

Preheat oven to 350°F. Empty contents of jar into a large mixing bowl, stirring to combine. Cut in shortening. Make a well in the center of mixture and add egg yolks, vanilla and almond extract. Beat on medium speed for 30 seconds until well combined. In another bowl, beat egg whites until soft peaks form. Gradually add sugar and continue beating until peaks are stiff but not dry. Fold egg whites into batter. Transfer to a greased 9 x 13 inch pan. Bake for 40 to 45 minutes.

Black Walnut Cake

1 jar Black Walnut Cake Mix	1/2 tsp. almond extract
3/4 C. shortening	1 C. whole milk
3 egg yolks	3 egg whites
1 tsp. vanilla	1/4 C. sugar

Preheat oven to 350°F. Empty contents of jar into a large mixing bowl, stirring to combine. Cut in shortening. Make a well in the center of mixture and add egg yolks, vanilla and almond extract. Beat on medium speed for 30 seconds until well combined. In another bowl, beat egg whites until soft peaks form. Gradually add sugar and continue beating until peaks are stiff but not dry. Fold egg whites into batter. Transfer to a greased 9 x 13 inch pan. Bake for 40 to 45 minutes.

Black Walnut Cake

1 jar Black Walnut Cake Mix	1/2 tsp. almond extract
3/4 C. shortening	1 C. whole milk
3 egg yolks	3 egg whites
1 tsp. vanilla	1/4 C. sugar

Preheat oven to 350°F. Empty contents of jar into a large mixing bowl, stirring to combine. Cut in shortening. Make a well in the center of mixture and add egg yolks, vanilla and almond extract. Beat on medium speed for 30 seconds until well combined. In another bowl, beat egg whites until soft peaks form. Gradually add sugar and continue beating until peaks are stiff but not dry. Fold egg whites into batter. Transfer to a greased 9 x 13 inch pan. Bake for 40 to 45 minutes.

Black Walnut Cake

1 jar Black Walnut Cake Mix	1/2 tsp. almond extract
3/4 C. shortening	1 C. whole milk
3 egg yolks	3 egg whites
1 tsp. vanilla	1/4 C. sugar

Preheat oven to 350°F. Empty contents of jar into a large mixing bowl, stirring to combine. Cut in shortening. Make a well in the center of mixture and add egg yolks, vanilla and almond extract. Beat on medium speed for 30 seconds until well combined. In another bowl, beat egg whites until soft peaks form. Gradually add sugar and continue beating until peaks are stiff but not dry. Fold egg whites into batter. Transfer to a greased 9 x 13 inch pan. Bake for 40 to 45 minutes.

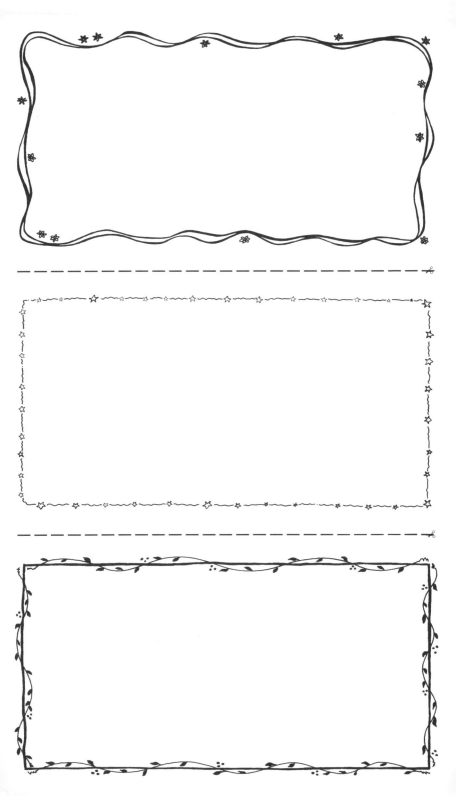

Black Walnut Cake

1 jar Black Walnut Cake Mix
3/4 C. shortening
3 egg yolks
1 tsp. vanilla

1/2 tsp. almond extract
1 C. whole milk
3 egg whites
1/4 C. sugar

Preheat oven to 350°F. Empty contents of jar into a large mixing bowl, stirring to combine. Cut in shortening. Make a well in the center of mixture and add egg yolks, vanilla and almond extract. Beat on medium speed for 30 seconds until well combined. In another bowl, beat egg whites until soft peaks form. Gradually add sugar and continue beating until peaks are stiff but not dry. Fold egg whites into batter. Transfer to a greased 9 x 13 inch pan. Bake for 40 to 45 minutes.

Black Walnut Cake

1 jar Black Walnut Cake Mix
3/4 C. shortening
3 egg yolks
1 tsp. vanilla

1/2 tsp. almond extract
1 C. whole milk
3 egg whites
1/4 C. sugar

Preheat oven to 350°F. Empty contents of jar into a large mixing bowl, stirring to combine. Cut in shortening. Make a well in the center of mixture and add egg yolks, vanilla and almond extract. Beat on medium speed for 30 seconds until well combined. In another bowl, beat egg whites until soft peaks form. Gradually add sugar and continue beating until peaks are stiff but not dry. Fold egg whites into batter. Transfer to a greased 9 x 13 inch pan. Bake for 40 to 45 minutes.

Black Walnut Cake

1 jar Black Walnut Cake Mix
3/4 C. shortening
3 egg yolks
1 tsp. vanilla

1/2 tsp. almond extract
1 C. whole milk
3 egg whites
1/4 C. sugar

Preheat oven to 350°F. Empty contents of jar into a large mixing bowl, stirring to combine. Cut in shortening. Make a well in the center of mixture and add egg yolks, vanilla and almond extract. Beat on medium speed for 30 seconds until well combined. In another bowl, beat egg whites until soft peaks form. Gradually add sugar and continue beating until peaks are stiff but not dry. Fold egg whites into batter. Transfer to a greased 9 x 13 inch pan. Bake for 40 to 45 minutes.

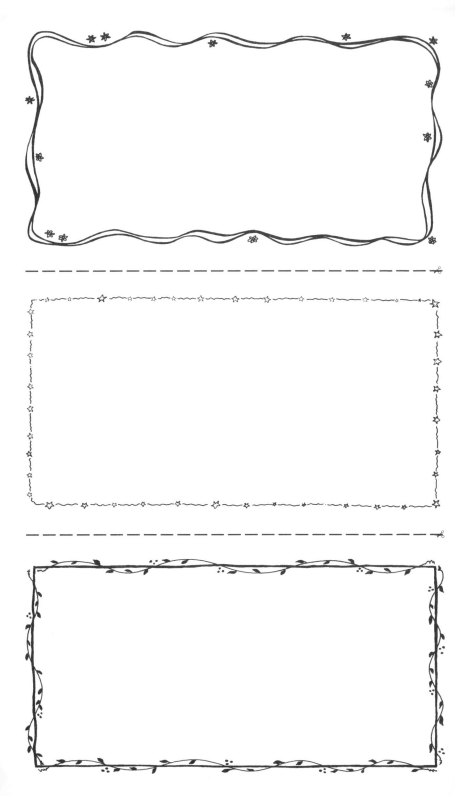

Moist Mocha Cake Mix

1 3/4 C. sugar
3/4 C. unsweetened cocoa
1 3/4 C. flour
2 tsp. baking soda
1 tsp. baking powder
1/2 tsp. salt

Layer the ingredients in the order given into a wide-mouth 1-quart canning jar. Pack each layer into place before adding the next ingredient.

Attach a gift tag with the mixing and baking instructions.

Moist Mocha Cake

1 jar Moist Mocha Cake Mix
2 eggs
3/4 C. strong brewed coffee
1 C. buttermilk
1/2 C. vegetable oil
1 tsp. vanilla

Preheat oven to 350°F. Empty contents of jar into a large mixing bowl, stirring to combine. Add eggs, coffee, buttermilk, oil and vanilla. Beat on medium speed for 2 minutes. Batter will be thin. Pour batter into a greased Bundt pan or tube pan. Bake for 45 to 50 minutes. Cool for 15 to 20 minutes before inverting onto a serving plate. Dust with powdered sugar.

Moist Mocha Cake

1 jar Moist Mocha Cake Mix
2 eggs
3/4 C. strong brewed coffee

1 C. buttermilk
1/2 C. vegetable oil
1 tsp. vanilla

Preheat oven to 350°F. Empty contents of jar into a large mixing bowl, stirring to combine. Add eggs, coffee, buttermilk, oil and vanilla. Beat on medium speed for 2 minutes. Batter will be thin. Pour batter into a greased Bundt pan or tube pan. Bake for 45 to 50 minutes. Cool for 15 to 20 minutes before inverting onto a serving plate. Dust with powdered sugar.

Moist Mocha Cake

1 jar Moist Mocha Cake Mix
2 eggs
3/4 C. strong brewed coffee

1 C. buttermilk
1/2 C. vegetable oil
1 tsp. vanilla

Preheat oven to 350°F. Empty contents of jar into a large mixing bowl, stirring to combine. Add eggs, coffee, buttermilk, oil and vanilla. Beat on medium speed for 2 minutes. Batter will be thin. Pour batter into a greased Bundt pan or tube pan. Bake for 45 to 50 minutes. Cool for 15 to 20 minutes before inverting onto a serving plate. Dust with powdered sugar.

Moist Mocha Cake

1 jar Moist Mocha Cake Mix
2 eggs
3/4 C. strong brewed coffee

1 C. buttermilk
1/2 C. vegetable oil
1 tsp. vanilla

Preheat oven to 350°F. Empty contents of jar into a large mixing bowl, stirring to combine. Add eggs, coffee, buttermilk, oil and vanilla. Beat on medium speed for 2 minutes. Batter will be thin. Pour batter into a greased Bundt pan or tube pan. Bake for 45 to 50 minutes. Cool for 15 to 20 minutes before inverting onto a serving plate. Dust with powdered sugar.

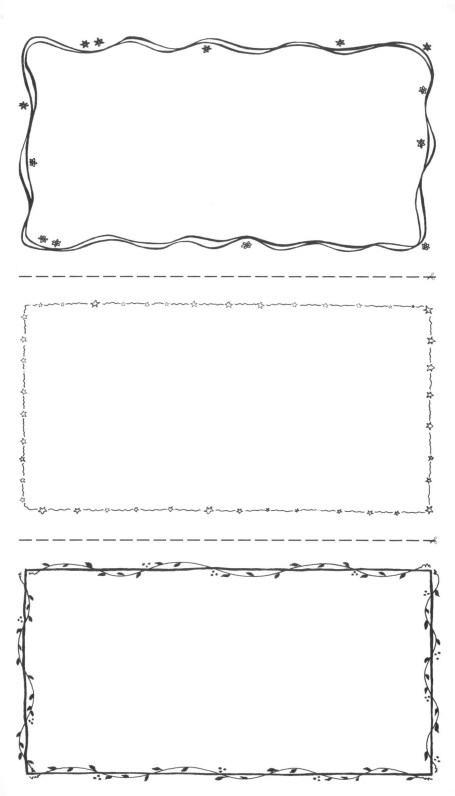

Moist Mocha Cake

1 jar Moist Mocha Cake Mix
2 eggs
3/4 C. strong brewed coffee

1 C. buttermilk
1/2 C. vegetable oil
1 tsp. vanilla

Preheat oven to 350°F. Empty contents of jar into a large mixing bowl, stirring to combine. Add eggs, coffee, buttermilk, oil and vanilla. Beat on medium speed for 2 minutes. Batter will be thin. Pour batter into a greased Bundt pan or tube pan. Bake for 45 to 50 minutes. Cool for 15 to 20 minutes before inverting onto a serving plate. Dust with powdered sugar.

Moist Mocha Cake

1 jar Moist Mocha Cake Mix
2 eggs
3/4 C. strong brewed coffee

1 C. buttermilk
1/2 C. vegetable oil
1 tsp. vanilla

Preheat oven to 350°F. Empty contents of jar into a large mixing bowl, stirring to combine. Add eggs, coffee, buttermilk, oil and vanilla. Beat on medium speed for 2 minutes. Batter will be thin. Pour batter into a greased Bundt pan or tube pan. Bake for 45 to 50 minutes. Cool for 15 to 20 minutes before inverting onto a serving plate. Dust with powdered sugar.

Moist Mocha Cake

1 jar Moist Mocha Cake Mix
2 eggs
3/4 C. strong brewed coffee

1 C. buttermilk
1/2 C. vegetable oil
1 tsp. vanilla

Preheat oven to 350°F. Empty contents of jar into a large mixing bowl, stirring to combine. Add eggs, coffee, buttermilk, oil and vanilla. Beat on medium speed for 2 minutes. Batter will be thin. Pour batter into a greased Bundt pan or tube pan. Bake for 45 to 50 minutes. Cool for 15 to 20 minutes before inverting onto a serving plate. Dust with powdered sugar.

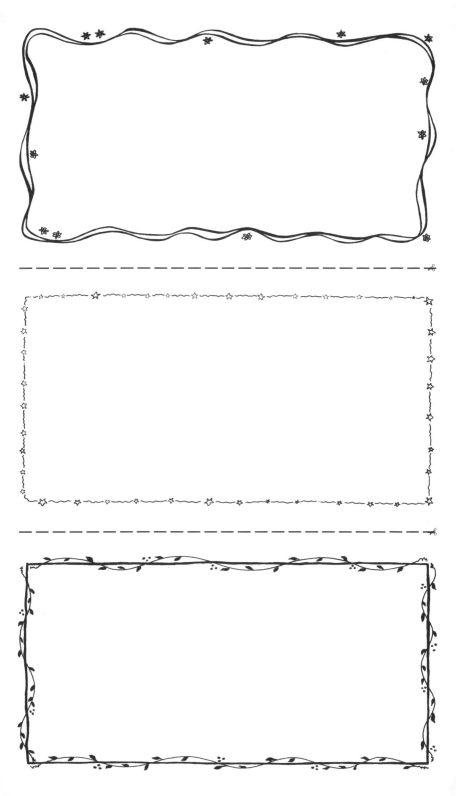

Chocolate Coffee Cake Mix

1/2 C. finely chopped pecans
1/2 C. currants
1 1/4 C. sugar
1 T. unsweetened cocoa
2 tsp. cinnamon
1/4 tsp. nutmeg
1 tsp. baking soda
1/2 tsp. baking powder
Pinch of salt
2 C. flour

Layer the ingredients in the order given into a wide-mouth 1-quart canning jar. Pack each layer into place before adding the next ingredient.

Attach a gift tag with the mixing and baking instructions.

❀ *Gifts in a Jar make great bake sale items.* ❀

Chocolate Coffee Cake

1 jar Chocolate Coffee Cake Mix
1 C. butter or margarine,
    softened
1 1/2 C. buttermilk

Preheat oven to 350°F. Empty contents of jar into a large mixing bowl, stirring to combine. Using a wire whisk cut in butter with dry ingredients until mixture resembles coarse crumbs. Set aside 2/3 C. for topping. Make a well in the center of the remaining crumb mixture and pour in buttermilk, stirring until just moistened. Transfer batter to a greased 9 x 13 inch pan. Sprinkle reserved crumb mixture over all. Bake for 30 to 35 minutes.

Chocolate Coffee Cake

1 jar Chocolate Coffee Cake Mix   1 1/2 C. buttermilk
1 C. butter or margarine, softened

Preheat oven to 350°F. Empty contents of jar into a large mixing bowl, stirring to combine. Using a wire whisk cut in butter with dry ingredients until mixture resembles coarse crumbs. Set aside 2/3 C. for topping. Make a well in the center of the remaining crumb mixture and pour in buttermilk, stirring until just moistened. Transfer batter to a greased 9 x 13 inch pan. Sprinkle reserved crumb mixture over all. Bake for 30 to 35 minutes.

Chocolate Coffee Cake

1 jar Chocolate Coffee Cake Mix   1 1/2 C. buttermilk
1 C. butter or margarine, softened

Preheat oven to 350°F. Empty contents of jar into a large mixing bowl, stirring to combine. Using a wire whisk cut in butter with dry ingredients until mixture resembles coarse crumbs. Set aside 2/3 C. for topping. Make a well in the center of the remaining crumb mixture and pour in buttermilk, stirring until just moistened. Transfer batter to a greased 9 x 13 inch pan. Sprinkle reserved crumb mixture over all. Bake for 30 to 35 minutes.

Chocolate Coffee Cake

1 jar Chocolate Coffee Cake Mix   1 1/2 C. buttermilk
1 C. butter or margarine, softened

Preheat oven to 350°F. Empty contents of jar into a large mixing bowl, stirring to combine. Using a wire whisk cut in butter with dry ingredients until mixture resembles coarse crumbs. Set aside 2/3 C. for topping. Make a well in the center of the remaining crumb mixture and pour in buttermilk, stirring until just moistened. Transfer batter to a greased 9 x 13 inch pan. Sprinkle reserved crumb mixture over all. Bake for 30 to 35 minutes.

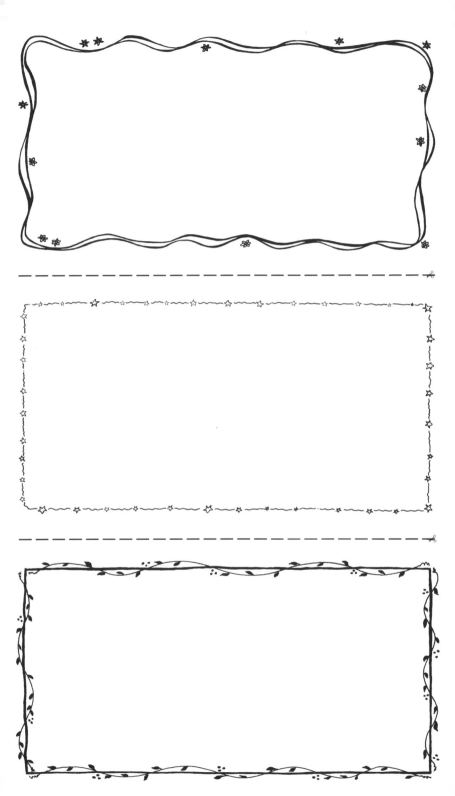

Chocolate Coffee Cake

1 jar Chocolate Coffee Cake Mix   1 1/2 C. buttermilk
1 C. butter or margarine, softened

Preheat oven to 350°F. Empty contents of jar into a large mixing bowl, stirring to combine. Using a wire whisk cut in butter with dry ingredients until mixture resembles coarse crumbs. Set aside 2/3 C. for topping. Make a well in the center of the remaining crumb mixture and pour in buttermilk, stirring until just moistened. Transfer batter to a greased 9 x 13 inch pan. Sprinkle reserved crumb mixture over all. Bake for 30 to 35 minutes.

Chocolate Coffee Cake

1 jar Chocolate Coffee Cake Mix   1 1/2 C. buttermilk
1 C. butter or margarine, softened

Preheat oven to 350°F. Empty contents of jar into a large mixing bowl, stirring to combine. Using a wire whisk cut in butter with dry ingredients until mixture resembles coarse crumbs. Set aside 2/3 C. for topping. Make a well in the center of the remaining crumb mixture and pour in buttermilk, stirring until just moistened. Transfer batter to a greased 9 x 13 inch pan. Sprinkle reserved crumb mixture over all. Bake for 30 to 35 minutes.

Chocolate Coffee Cake

1 jar Chocolate Coffee Cake Mix   1 1/2 C. buttermilk
1 C. butter or margarine, softened

Preheat oven to 350°F. Empty contents of jar into a large mixing bowl, stirring to combine. Using a wire whisk cut in butter with dry ingredients until mixture resembles coarse crumbs. Set aside 2/3 C. for topping. Make a well in the center of the remaining crumb mixture and pour in buttermilk, stirring until just moistened. Transfer batter to a greased 9 x 13 inch pan. Sprinkle reserved crumb mixture over all. Bake for 30 to 35 minutes.

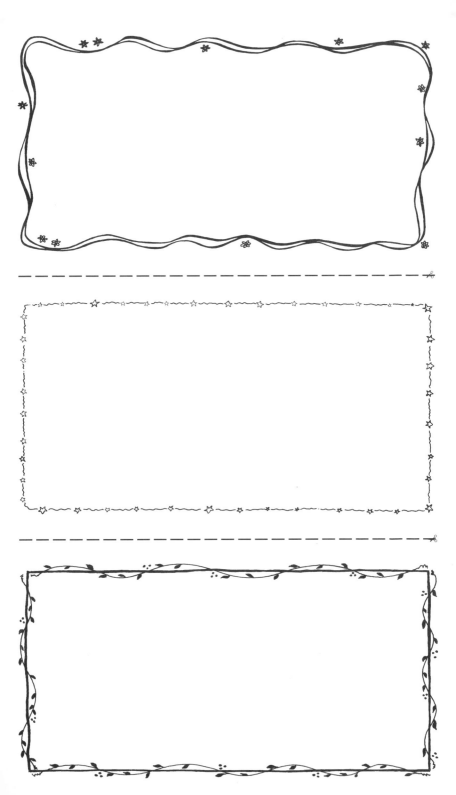

Carrot Cake Mix

3/4 C. finely chopped walnuts or
  pecans
1/2 C. golden raisins
1/2 C. raisins
1 1/3 C. flour
1 tsp. cinnamon
1/2 tsp. cloves
1/2 tsp. nutmeg
1/2 tsp. allspice
1/2 tsp. salt
1 1/2 tsp. baking powder
1 C. sugar

Layer the ingredients in the order given into a wide-mouth 1-quart canning jar. Pack each layer into place before adding the next ingredient.

Attach a gift tag with the mixing and baking instructions.

Carrot Cake

1 jar Carrot Cake Mix
2/3 C. vegetable oil
3 eggs
1 1/2 C. finely grated carrots
1/2 C. crushed pineapple, lightly
   drained (optional)

Preheat oven to 350°F. Empty contents of jar into a large mixing bowl, stirring to combine. Make a well in the center of dry ingredients and add oil and eggs. Mix until well combined. Stir in carrots and pineapple. Scrape batter into two greased 9 inch round pans or a 9 x 13 inch pan. Bake for 25 to 30 minutes in round pans or 30 to 35 in 9 x 13 inch pan.

Carrot Cake

1 jar Carrot Cake Mix
2/3 C. vegetable oil
3 eggs

1 1/2 C. finely grated carrots
1/2 C. crushed pineapple, lightly
    drained (optional)

Preheat oven to 350°F. Empty contents of jar into a large mixing bowl, stirring to combine. Make a well in the center of dry ingredients and add oil and eggs. Mix until well combined. Stir in carrots and pineapple. Scrape batter into two greased 9 inch round pans or a 9 x 13 inch pan. Bake for 25 to 30 minutes in round pans or 30 to 35 in 9 x 13 inch pan.

Carrot Cake

1 jar Carrot Cake Mix
2/3 C. vegetable oil
3 eggs

1 1/2 C. finely grated carrots
1/2 C. crushed pineapple, lightly
    drained (optional)

Preheat oven to 350°F. Empty contents of jar into a large mixing bowl, stirring to combine. Make a well in the center of dry ingredients and add oil and eggs. Mix until well combined. Stir in carrots and pineapple. Scrape batter into two greased 9 inch round pans or a 9 x 13 inch pan. Bake for 25 to 30 minutes in round pans or 30 to 35 in 9 x 13 inch pan.

Carrot Cake

1 jar Carrot Cake Mix
2/3 C. vegetable oil
3 eggs

1 1/2 C. finely grated carrots
1/2 C. crushed pineapple, lightly
    drained (optional)

Preheat oven to 350°F. Empty contents of jar into a large mixing bowl, stirring to combine. Make a well in the center of dry ingredients and add oil and eggs. Mix until well combined. Stir in carrots and pineapple. Scrape batter into two greased 9 inch round pans or a 9 x 13 inch pan. Bake for 25 to 30 minutes in round pans or 30 to 35 in 9 x 13 inch pan.

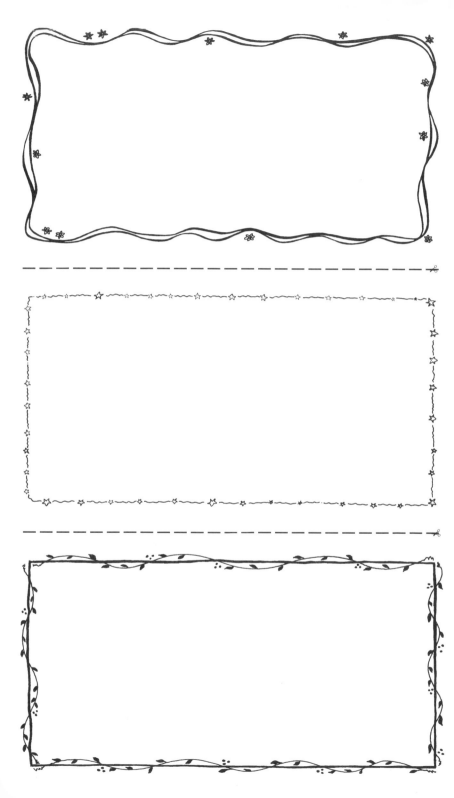

Carrot Cake

1 jar Carrot Cake Mix
2/3 C. vegetable oil
3 eggs

1 1/2 C. finely grated carrots
1/2 C. crushed pineapple, lightly
    drained (optional)

Preheat oven to 350°F. Empty contents of jar into a large mixing bowl, stirring to combine. Make a well in the center of dry ingredients and add oil and eggs. Mix until well combined. Stir in carrots and pineapple. Scrape batter into two greased 9 inch round pans or a 9 x 13 inch pan. Bake for 25 to 30 minutes in round pans or 30 to 35 in 9 x 13 inch pan.

Carrot Cake

1 jar Carrot Cake Mix
2/3 C. vegetable oil
3 eggs

1 1/2 C. finely grated carrots
1/2 C. crushed pineapple, lightly
    drained (optional)

Preheat oven to 350°F. Empty contents of jar into a large mixing bowl, stirring to combine. Make a well in the center of dry ingredients and add oil and eggs. Mix until well combined. Stir in carrots and pineapple. Scrape batter into two greased 9 inch round pans or a 9 x 13 inch pan. Bake for 25 to 30 minutes in round pans or 30 to 35 in 9 x 13 inch pan.

Carrot Cake

1 jar Carrot Cake Mix
2/3 C. vegetable oil
3 eggs

1 1/2 C. finely grated carrots
1/2 C. crushed pineapple, lightly
    drained (optional)

Preheat oven to 350°F. Empty contents of jar into a large mixing bowl, stirring to combine. Make a well in the center of dry ingredients and add oil and eggs. Mix until well combined. Stir in carrots and pineapple. Scrape batter into two greased 9 inch round pans or a 9 x 13 inch pan. Bake for 25 to 30 minutes in round pans or 30 to 35 in 9 x 13 inch pan.

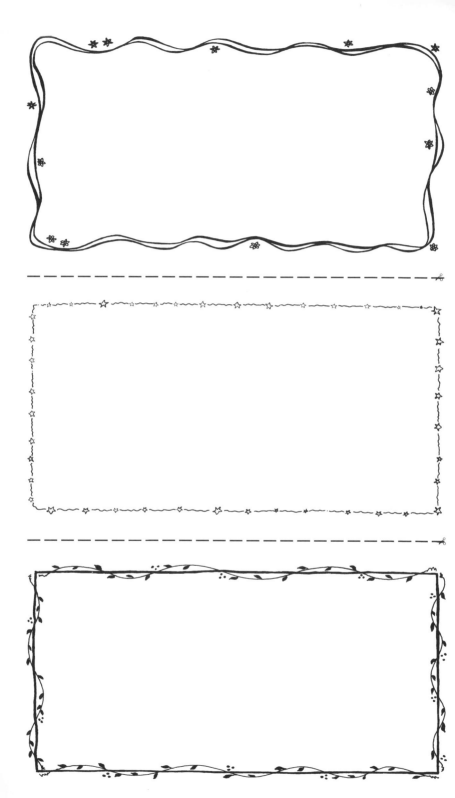

German Apple Cake Mix

1 3/4 C. sugar
1 1/4 C. chopped walnuts
1 1/4 C. flour
2 1/4 tsp. baking powder
1/2 tsp. salt

Layer the ingredients in the order given into a wide-mouth 1-quart canning jar. Pack each layer into place before adding the next ingredient.

Attach a gift tag with the mixing and baking instructions.

German Apple Cake

1 jar German Apple Cake Mix
5 eggs
1/2 C. vegetable oil
1 1/2 tsp. vanilla
3 tart apples, peeled &
   chopped

Preheat oven to 375°F. Empty contents of jar into a large mixing bowl, stirring to combine. Add eggs, oil and vanilla and mix well. Stir in chopped apples. Transfer batter to two greased 9 inch round pans or a 9 x 13 inch pan. Bake for 25 to 30 minutes in round pans or 35 to 40 in 9 x 13 inch pan.

German Apple Cake

1 jar German Apple Cake Mix
5 eggs
1/2 C. vegetable oil

1 1/2 tsp. vanilla
3 tart apples, peeled &
   chopped

Preheat oven to 375°F. Empty contents of jar into a large mixing bowl, stirring to combine. Add eggs, oil and vanilla and mix well. Stir in chopped apples. Transfer batter to two greased 9 inch round pans or a 9 x 13 inch pan. Bake for 25 to 30 minutes in round pans or 35 to 40 in 9 x 13 inch pan.

German Apple Cake

1 jar German Apple Cake Mix
5 eggs
1/2 C. vegetable oil

1 1/2 tsp. vanilla
3 tart apples, peeled &
   chopped

Preheat oven to 375°F. Empty contents of jar into a large mixing bowl, stirring to combine. Add eggs, oil and vanilla and mix well. Stir in chopped apples. Transfer batter to two greased 9 inch round pans or a 9 x 13 inch pan. Bake for 25 to 30 minutes in round pans or 35 to 40 in 9 x 13 inch pan.

German Apple Cake

1 jar German Apple Cake Mix
5 eggs
1/2 C. vegetable oil

1 1/2 tsp. vanilla
3 tart apples, peeled &
   chopped

Preheat oven to 375°F. Empty contents of jar into a large mixing bowl, stirring to combine. Add eggs, oil and vanilla and mix well. Stir in chopped apples. Transfer batter to two greased 9 inch round pans or a 9 x 13 inch pan. Bake for 25 to 30 minutes in round pans or 35 to 40 in 9 x 13 inch pan.

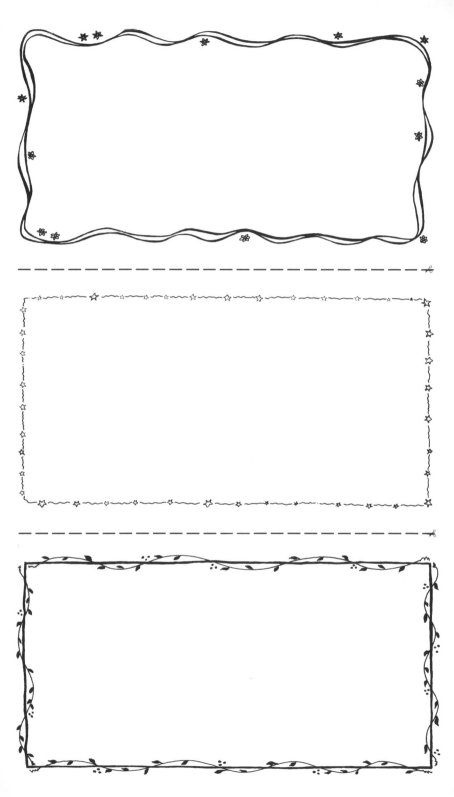

German Apple Cake

1 jar German Apple Cake Mix
5 eggs
1/2 C. vegetable oil

1 1/2 tsp. vanilla
3 tart apples, peeled &
   chopped

   Preheat oven to 375°F. Empty contents of jar into a large mixing bowl, stirring to combine. Add eggs, oil and vanilla and mix well. Stir in chopped apples. Transfer batter to two greased 9 inch round pans or a 9 x 13 inch pan. Bake for 25 to 30 minutes in round pans or 35 to 40 in 9 x 13 inch pan.

German Apple Cake

1 jar German Apple Cake Mix
5 eggs
1/2 C. vegetable oil

1 1/2 tsp. vanilla
3 tart apples, peeled &
   chopped

   Preheat oven to 375°F. Empty contents of jar into a large mixing bowl, stirring to combine. Add eggs, oil and vanilla and mix well. Stir in chopped apples. Transfer batter to two greased 9 inch round pans or a 9 x 13 inch pan. Bake for 25 to 30 minutes in round pans or 35 to 40 in 9 x 13 inch pan.

German Apple Cake

1 jar German Apple Cake Mix
5 eggs
1/2 C. vegetable oil

1 1/2 tsp. vanilla
3 tart apples, peeled &
   chopped

   Preheat oven to 375°F. Empty contents of jar into a large mixing bowl, stirring to combine. Add eggs, oil and vanilla and mix well. Stir in chopped apples. Transfer batter to two greased 9 inch round pans or a 9 x 13 inch pan. Bake for 25 to 30 minutes in round pans or 35 to 40 in 9 x 13 inch pan.

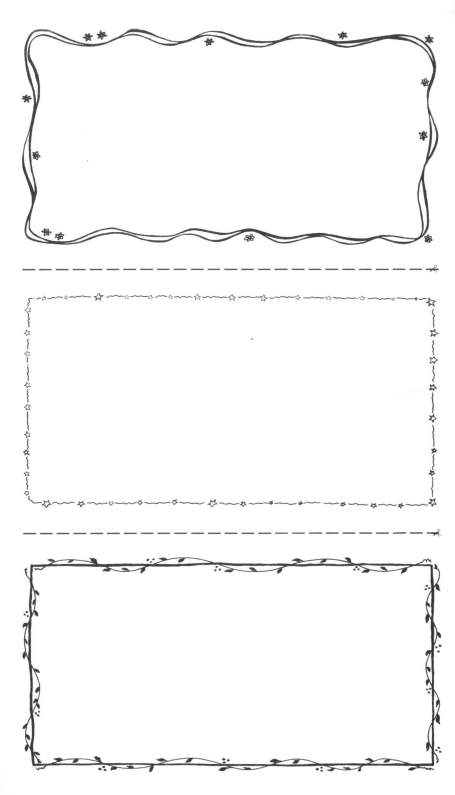

Peach Cobbler Mix

3/4 C. sugar
3/4 C. sliced almonds or pecans,
   toasted*
2 2/3 C. flour
2 tsp. baking powder
1 tsp. baking soda

Layer the ingredients in the order given into a wide-mouth 1-quart canning jar. Pack each layer into place before adding the next ingredient.

Attach a gift tag with the mixing and baking instructions.

*To toast, place nuts in a single layer on a baking sheet. Bake at 350°F for approximately 10 minutes or until nuts are golden brown.

❀ At times, it may seem impossible to make all of the jar ingredients fit, but with persistence, they do all fit. ❀

Peach Cobbler

1 jar Peach Cobbler Mix
8 ripe peaches, sliced (may use
  frozen, approx. 8 cups)
2/3 C. sugar
3/4 C. butter or margarine, cold
1 C. sour cream
3/4 C. whole milk or cream

Preheat oven to 350°F. Spread peach slices evenly over the bottom of a greased 7 x 11 inch pan. Sprinkle sugar over the top. Empty contents of jar into a mixing bowl, stirring to combine. Cut butter into dry ingredients. Make a well in the center and add sour cream and milk. Stir to combine then knead against the sides of the bowl 5 to 10 times. Transfer to a floured surface and roll out to 1/4 to 1/2" thickness. Cut dough into circles or squares and place over sliced peaches. Bake for 50 to 55 minutes.

Peach Cobbler

1 jar Peach Cobbler Mix
8 ripe peaches, sliced (may use
   frozen, approx. 8 cups)
2/3 C. sugar

3/4 C. butter or margarine,
   cold
1 C. sour cream
3/4 C. whole milk or cream

Preheat oven to 350°F. Spread peach slices evenly over the bottom of a greased 7 x 11 inch pan. Sprinkle sugar over the top. Empty contents of jar into a mixing bowl, stirring to combine. Cut butter into dry ingredients. Make a well in the center and add sour cream and milk. Stir to combine then knead against the sides of the bowl 5 to 10 times. Transfer to a floured surface and roll out to 1/4 to 1/2" thickness. Cut dough into circles or squares and place over sliced peaches. Bake for 50 to 55 minutes.

Peach Cobbler

1 jar Peach Cobbler Mix
8 ripe peaches, sliced (may use
   frozen, approx. 8 cups)
2/3 C. sugar

3/4 C. butter or margarine,
   cold
1 C. sour cream
3/4 C. whole milk or cream

Preheat oven to 350°F. Spread peach slices evenly over the bottom of a greased 7 x 11 inch pan. Sprinkle sugar over the top. Empty contents of jar into a mixing bowl, stirring to combine. Cut butter into dry ingredients. Make a well in the center and add sour cream and milk. Stir to combine then knead against the sides of the bowl 5 to 10 times. Transfer to a floured surface and roll out to 1/4 to 1/2" thickness. Cut dough into circles or squares and place over sliced peaches. Bake for 50 to 55 minutes.

Peach Cobbler

1 jar Peach Cobbler Mix
8 ripe peaches, sliced (may use
   frozen, approx. 8 cups)
2/3 C. sugar

3/4 C. butter or margarine,
   cold
1 C. sour cream
3/4 C. whole milk or cream

Preheat oven to 350°F. Spread peach slices evenly over the bottom of a greased 7 x 11 inch pan. Sprinkle sugar over the top. Empty contents of jar into a mixing bowl, stirring to combine. Cut butter into dry ingredients. Make a well in the center and add sour cream and milk. Stir to combine then knead against the sides of the bowl 5 to 10 times. Transfer to a floured surface and roll out to 1/4 to 1/2" thickness. Cut dough into circles or squares and place over sliced peaches. Bake for 50 to 55 minutes.

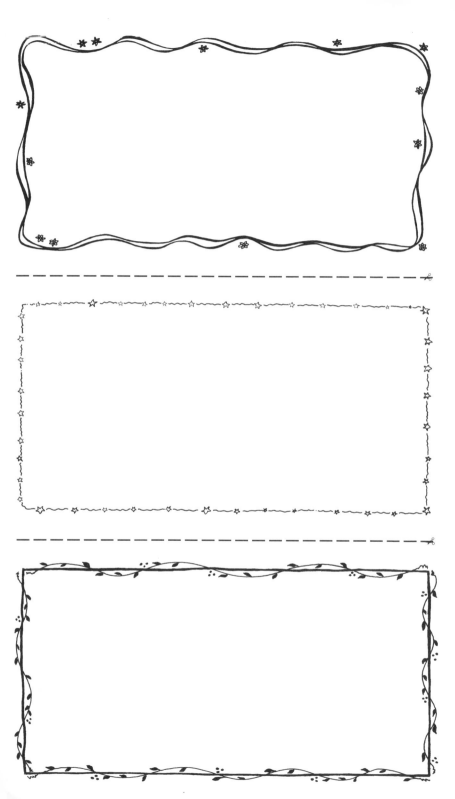

Peach Cobbler

1 jar Peach Cobbler Mix
8 ripe peaches, sliced (may use
  frozen, approx. 8 cups)
2/3 C. sugar

3/4 C. butter or margarine,
  cold
1 C. sour cream
3/4 C. whole milk or cream

Preheat oven to 350°F. Spread peach slices evenly over the bottom of a greased 7 x 11 inch pan. Sprinkle sugar over the top. Empty contents of jar into a mixing bowl, stirring to combine. Cut butter into dry ingredients. Make a well in the center and add sour cream and milk. Stir to combine then knead against the sides of the bowl 5 to 10 times. Transfer to a floured surface and roll out to 1/4 to 1/2" thickness. Cut dough into circles or squares and place over sliced peaches. Bake for 50 to 55 minutes.

Peach Cobbler

1 jar Peach Cobbler Mix
8 ripe peaches, sliced (may use
  frozen, approx. 8 cups)
2/3 C. sugar

3/4 C. butter or margarine,
  cold
1 C. sour cream
3/4 C. whole milk or cream

Preheat oven to 350°F. Spread peach slices evenly over the bottom of a greased 7 x 11 inch pan. Sprinkle sugar over the top. Empty contents of jar into a mixing bowl, stirring to combine. Cut butter into dry ingredients. Make a well in the center and add sour cream and milk. Stir to combine then knead against the sides of the bowl 5 to 10 times. Transfer to a floured surface and roll out to 1/4 to 1/2" thickness. Cut dough into circles or squares and place over sliced peaches. Bake for 50 to 55 minutes.

Peach Cobbler

1 jar Peach Cobbler Mix
8 ripe peaches, sliced (may use
  frozen, approx. 8 cups)
2/3 C. sugar

3/4 C. butter or margarine,
  cold
1 C. sour cream
3/4 C. whole milk or cream

Preheat oven to 350°F. Spread peach slices evenly over the bottom of a greased 7 x 11 inch pan. Sprinkle sugar over the top. Empty contents of jar into a mixing bowl, stirring to combine. Cut butter into dry ingredients. Make a well in the center and add sour cream and milk. Stir to combine then knead against the sides of the bowl 5 to 10 times. Transfer to a floured surface and roll out to 1/4 to 1/2" thickness. Cut dough into circles or squares and place over sliced peaches. Bake for 50 to 55 minutes.

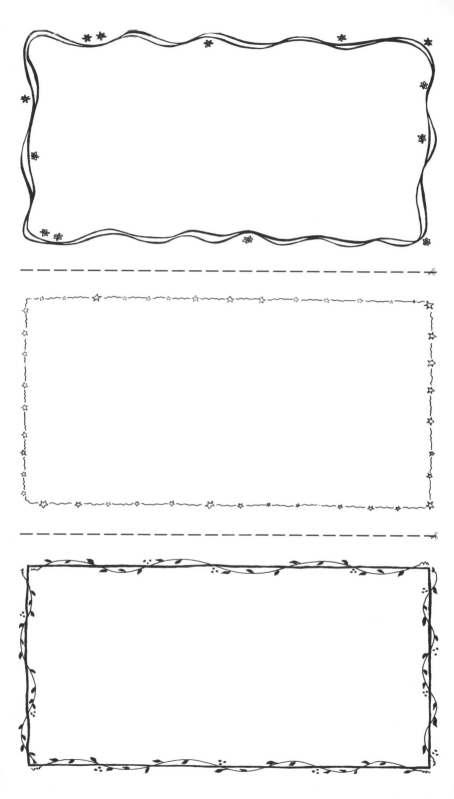

Coconut Pineapple Pudding Cake Mix

2/3 C. white chocolate chips
2/3 C. coconut
1 (3.4 oz.) pkg. vanilla pudding
3/4 C. sugar
1 3/4 C. flour
2 tsp. baking powder
1/2 tsp. baking soda
1/2 tsp. salt

Layer the ingredients in the order given into a wide-mouth 1-quart canning jar. Pack each layer into place before adding the next ingredient.

Attach a gift tag with the mixing and baking instructions.

Coconut Pineapple Pudding Cake

1 jar Coconut Pineapple Pudding
   Cake Mix
2/3 C. shortening
2 eggs
2/3 C. milk
1/2 C. crushed pineapple, lightly
   drained

Preheat oven to 350°F. Empty contents of jar into a mixing bowl, stirring to combine. Cut shortening into dry ingredients. Make a well in the center and add eggs and milk. Mix on low speed for 3 minutes. Stir in pineapple. Pour batter into greased Bundt pan or tube pan. Bake for 50 minutes.

Coconut Pineapple Pudding Cake

1 jar Coconut Pineapple Pudding
   Cake Mix
2/3 C. shortening
2 eggs

2/3 C. milk
1/2 C. crushed pineapple,
   lightly drained

    Preheat oven to 350°F. Empty contents of jar into a mixing bowl, stirring to combine. Cut shortening into dry ingredients. Make a well in the center and add eggs and milk. Mix on low speed for 3 minutes. Stir in pineapple. Pour batter into greased Bundt pan or tube pan. Bake for 50 minutes.

Coconut Pineapple Pudding Cake

1 jar Coconut Pineapple Pudding
   Cake Mix
2/3 C. shortening
2 eggs

2/3 C. milk
1/2 C. crushed pineapple,
   lightly drained

    Preheat oven to 350°F. Empty contents of jar into a mixing bowl, stirring to combine. Cut shortening into dry ingredients. Make a well in the center and add eggs and milk. Mix on low speed for 3 minutes. Stir in pineapple. Pour batter into greased Bundt pan or tube pan. Bake for 50 minutes.

Coconut Pineapple Pudding Cake

1 jar Coconut Pineapple Pudding
   Cake Mix
2/3 C. shortening
2 eggs

2/3 C. milk
1/2 C. crushed pineapple,
   lightly drained

    Preheat oven to 350°F. Empty contents of jar into a mixing bowl, stirring to combine. Cut shortening into dry ingredients. Make a well in the center and add eggs and milk. Mix on low speed for 3 minutes. Stir in pineapple. Pour batter into greased Bundt pan or tube pan. Bake for 50 minutes.

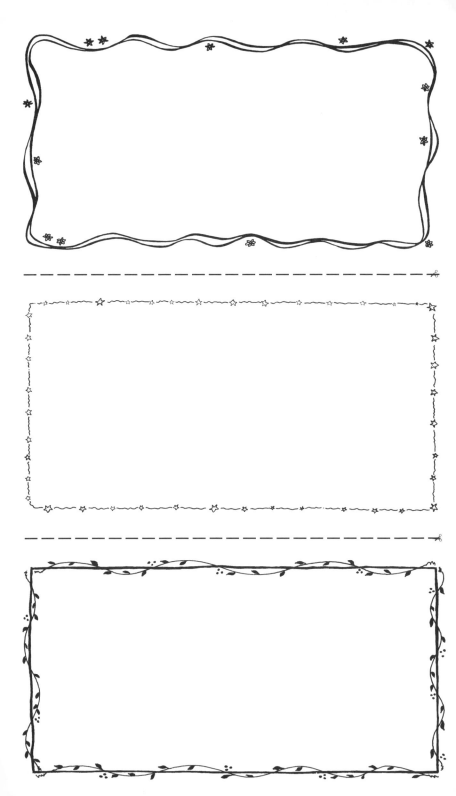

Coconut Pineapple Pudding Cake

1 jar Coconut Pineapple Pudding
   Cake Mix
2/3 C. shortening
2 eggs

2/3 C. milk
1/2 C. crushed pineapple,
   lightly drained

   Preheat oven to 350°F. Empty contents of jar into a mixing bowl, stirring to combine. Cut shortening into dry ingredients. Make a well in the center and add eggs and milk. Mix on low speed for 3 minutes. Stir in pineapple. Pour batter into greased Bundt pan or tube pan. Bake for 50 minutes.

Coconut Pineapple Pudding Cake

1 jar Coconut Pineapple Pudding
   Cake Mix
2/3 C. shortening
2 eggs

2/3 C. milk
1/2 C. crushed pineapple,
   lightly drained

   Preheat oven to 350°F. Empty contents of jar into a mixing bowl, stirring to combine. Cut shortening into dry ingredients. Make a well in the center and add eggs and milk. Mix on low speed for 3 minutes. Stir in pineapple. Pour batter into greased Bundt pan or tube pan. Bake for 50 minutes.

Coconut Pineapple Pudding Cake

1 jar Coconut Pineapple Pudding
   Cake Mix
2/3 C. shortening
2 eggs

2/3 C. milk
1/2 C. crushed pineapple,
   lightly drained

   Preheat oven to 350°F. Empty contents of jar into a mixing bowl, stirring to combine. Cut shortening into dry ingredients. Make a well in the center and add eggs and milk. Mix on low speed for 3 minutes. Stir in pineapple. Pour batter into greased Bundt pan or tube pan. Bake for 50 minutes.

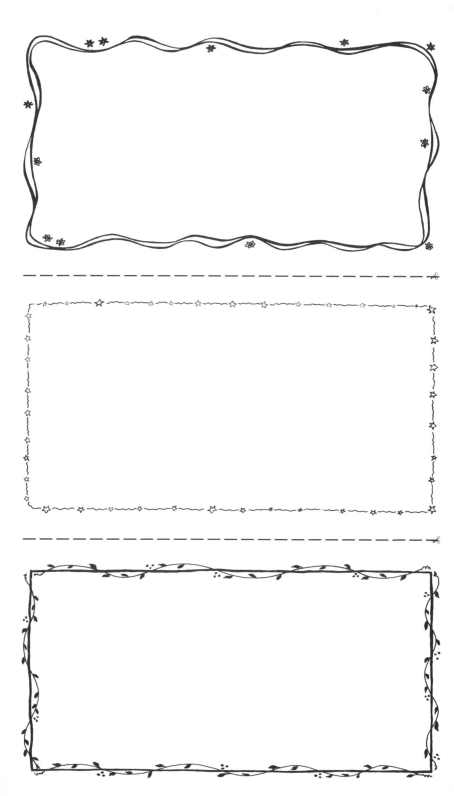

Caramel-Pecan Upside Down Cake Mix

3/4 C. sugar
1 1/2 tsp. baking powder
1/2 tsp. salt
1 1/2 C. flour

Topping Packet:
3/4 C. brown sugar
1 C. pecans, coarsely chopped

Layer the ingredients in the order given into a wide-mouth 1-quart canning jar. Pack each layer into place before adding the next ingredient. Mix and place the brown sugar and pecans in a small plastic bag. Place the packet on top of the flour.

Attach a gift tag with the mixing and baking instructions.

Caramel-Pecan Upside Down Cake

1 jar Caramel-Pecan Upside
    Down Cake Mix
1/3 C. butter or margarine
1/3 C. corn syrup
3/4 C. shortening
2 eggs
1 C. milk
1 tsp. vanilla

Preheat oven to 350°F. Remove pecan packet from jar. Place packet contents in saucepan and cook with butter and corn syrup until sugar is dissolved. Spoon the mixture into a greased 7 x 11 inch pan or 9 inch round pan. Empty remaining contents of jar into a mixing bowl, stirring to combine. Cut shortening into dry ingredients. Make a well in the center and add eggs, milk and vanilla. Mix on low speed for 1 minute, scrape bowl sides then mix on medium speed for another 2 minutes. Pour batter over pecan and caramel mixture. Bake for 30 minutes. Cool cake for 5 minutes before inverting onto serving plate.

Caramel-Pecan Upside Down Cake

1 jar Caramel-Pecan Upside
   Down Cake Mix
1/3 C. butter or margarine
1/3 C. corn syrup

3/4 C. shortening
2 eggs
1 C. milk
1 tsp. vanilla

Preheat oven to 350°F. Remove pecan packet from jar. Place packet contents in saucepan and cook with butter and corn syrup until sugar is dissolved. Spoon the mixture into a greased 7 x 11 inch pan or 9 inch round pan. Empty remaining contents of jar into a mixing bowl, stirring to combine. Cut shortening into dry ingredients. Make a well in the center and add eggs, milk and vanilla. Mix on low speed for 1 minute, scrape bowl sides then mix on medium speed for another 2 minutes. Pour batter over pecan and caramel mixture. Bake for 30 minutes. Cool cake for 5 minutes before inverting onto serving plate.

Caramel-Pecan Upside Down Cake

1 jar Caramel-Pecan Upside
   Down Cake Mix
1/3 C. butter or margarine
1/3 C. corn syrup

3/4 C. shortening
2 eggs
1 C. milk
1 tsp. vanilla

Preheat oven to 350°F. Remove pecan packet from jar. Place packet contents in saucepan and cook with butter and corn syrup until sugar is dissolved. Spoon the mixture into a greased 7 x 11 inch pan or 9 inch round pan. Empty remaining contents of jar into a mixing bowl, stirring to combine. Cut shortening into dry ingredients. Make a well in the center and add eggs, milk and vanilla. Mix on low speed for 1 minute, scrape bowl sides then mix on medium speed for another 2 minutes. Pour batter over pecan and caramel mixture. Bake for 30 minutes. Cool cake for 5 minutes before inverting onto serving plate.

Caramel-Pecan Upside Down Cake

1 jar Caramel-Pecan Upside
   Down Cake Mix
1/3 C. butter or margarine
1/3 C. corn syrup

3/4 C. shortening
2 eggs
1 C. milk
1 tsp. vanilla

Preheat oven to 350°F. Remove pecan packet from jar. Place packet contents in saucepan and cook with butter and corn syrup until sugar is dissolved. Spoon the mixture into a greased 7 x 11 inch pan or 9 inch round pan. Empty remaining contents of jar into a mixing bowl, stirring to combine. Cut shortening into dry ingredients. Make a well in the center and add eggs, milk and vanilla. Mix on low speed for 1 minute, scrape bowl sides then mix on medium speed for another 2 minutes. Pour batter over pecan and caramel mixture. Bake for 30 minutes. Cool cake for 5 minutes before inverting onto serving plate.

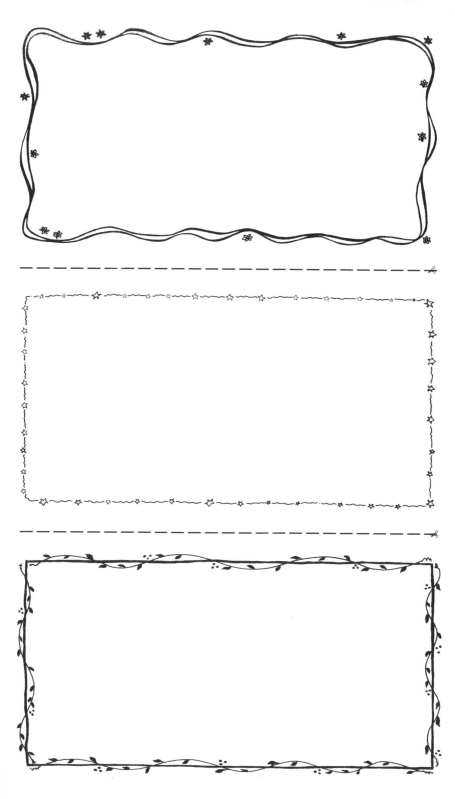

Caramel-Pecan Upside Down Cake

1 jar Caramel-Pecan Upside
   Down Cake Mix
1/3 C. butter or margarine
1/3 C. corn syrup

3/4 C. shortening
2 eggs
1 C. milk
1 tsp. vanilla

   Preheat oven to 350°F. Remove pecan packet from jar. Place packet contents in saucepan and cook with butter and corn syrup until sugar is dissolved. Spoon the mixture into a greased 7 x 11 inch pan or 9 inch round pan. Empty remaining contents of jar into a mixing bowl, stirring to combine. Cut shortening into dry ingredients. Make a well in the center and add eggs, milk and vanilla. Mix on low speed for 1 minute, scrape bowl sides then mix on medium speed for another 2 minutes. Pour batter over pecan and caramel mixture. Bake for 30 minutes. Cool cake for 5 minutes before inverting onto serving plate.

Caramel-Pecan Upside Down Cake

1 jar Caramel-Pecan Upside
   Down Cake Mix
1/3 C. butter or margarine
1/3 C. corn syrup

3/4 C. shortening
2 eggs
1 C. milk
1 tsp. vanilla

   Preheat oven to 350°F. Remove pecan packet from jar. Place packet contents in saucepan and cook with butter and corn syrup until sugar is dissolved. Spoon the mixture into a greased 7 x 11 inch pan or 9 inch round pan. Empty remaining contents of jar into a mixing bowl, stirring to combine. Cut shortening into dry ingredients. Make a well in the center and add eggs, milk and vanilla. Mix on low speed for 1 minute, scrape bowl sides then mix on medium speed for another 2 minutes. Pour batter over pecan and caramel mixture. Bake for 30 minutes. Cool cake for 5 minutes before inverting onto serving plate.

Caramel-Pecan Upside Down Cake

1 jar Caramel-Pecan Upside
   Down Cake Mix
1/3 C. butter or margarine
1/3 C. corn syrup

3/4 C. shortening
2 eggs
1 C. milk
1 tsp. vanilla

   Preheat oven to 350°F. Remove pecan packet from jar. Place packet contents in saucepan and cook with butter and corn syrup until sugar is dissolved. Spoon the mixture into a greased 7 x 11 inch pan or 9 inch round pan. Empty remaining contents of jar into a mixing bowl, stirring to combine. Cut shortening into dry ingredients. Make a well in the center and add eggs, milk and vanilla. Mix on low speed for 1 minute, scrape bowl sides then mix on medium speed for another 2 minutes. Pour batter over pecan and caramel mixture. Bake for 30 minutes. Cool cake for 5 minutes before inverting onto serving plate.

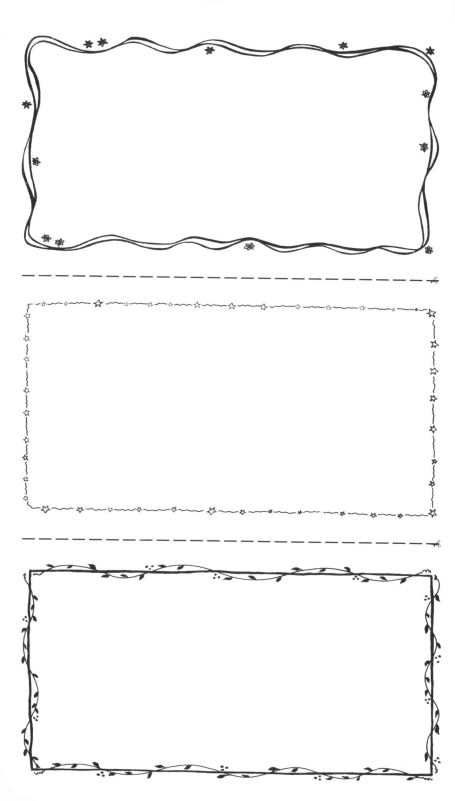

Raisin Spice Cake Mix

1/2 C. chopped walnuts or
    pecans
1 1/4 C. raisins
1 C. brown sugar
1 tsp. cinnamon
1/2 tsp. cloves
1/2 tsp. nutmeg
1/2 tsp. salt
1 tsp. baking soda
1 1/2 C. flour

Layer the ingredients in the order given into a wide-mouth 1-quart canning jar. Pack each layer into place before adding the next ingredient.

Attach a gift tag with the mixing and baking instructions.

❀ For an out of the ordinary gift, try placing the mix in a mixing bowl along with kitchen utensils, cookbooks, recipe cards, towels, potholders, and cookie cutters. ❀

Raisin Spice Cake

1 jar Raisin Spice Cake Mix
1 C. buttermilk
1/2 C. vegetable oil
1 tsp. vanilla
2 T. rum or brandy

Preheat the oven to 350°F. Empty contents of jar into a mixing bowl, stirring to combine. Add buttermilk, oil, vanilla and rum or brandy. Stir well until the mixture is well blended. Pour batter into a greased 7 x 11 inch pan or 9 inch round pan. Bake for 35 to 40 minutes. If desired, make a frosting by whipping 1/2 C. shortening with 2 C. powdered sugar then add 1 tsp. vanilla and 3 to 4 T. milk and continue to whip until fluffy.

Raisin Spice Cake

1 jar Raisin Spice Cake Mix
1 C. buttermilk
1/2 C. vegetable oil

1 tsp. vanilla
2 T. rum or brandy

Preheat the oven to 350°F. Empty contents of jar into a mixing bowl, stirring to combine. Add buttermilk, oil, vanilla and rum or brandy. Stir well until the mixture is well blended. Pour batter into a greased 7 x 11 inch pan or 9 inch round pan. Bake for 35 to 40 minutes. If desired, make a frosting by whipping 1/2 C. shortening with 2 C. powdered sugar then add 1 tsp. vanilla and 3 to 4 T. milk and continue to whip until fluffy.

Raisin Spice Cake

1 jar Raisin Spice Cake Mix
1 C. buttermilk
1/2 C. vegetable oil

1 tsp. vanilla
2 T. rum or brandy

Preheat the oven to 350°F. Empty contents of jar into a mixing bowl, stirring to combine. Add buttermilk, oil, vanilla and rum or brandy. Stir well until the mixture is well blended. Pour batter into a greased 7 x 11 inch pan or 9 inch round pan. Bake for 35 to 40 minutes. If desired, make a frosting by whipping 1/2 C. shortening with 2 C. powdered sugar then add 1 tsp. vanilla and 3 to 4 T. milk and continue to whip until fluffy.

Raisin Spice Cake

1 jar Raisin Spice Cake Mix
1 C. buttermilk
1/2 C. vegetable oil

1 tsp. vanilla
2 T. rum or brandy

Preheat the oven to 350°F. Empty contents of jar into a mixing bowl, stirring to combine. Add buttermilk, oil, vanilla and rum or brandy. Stir well until the mixture is well blended. Pour batter into a greased 7 x 11 inch pan or 9 inch round pan. Bake for 35 to 40 minutes. If desired, make a frosting by whipping 1/2 C. shortening with 2 C. powdered sugar then add 1 tsp. vanilla and 3 to 4 T. milk and continue to whip until fluffy.

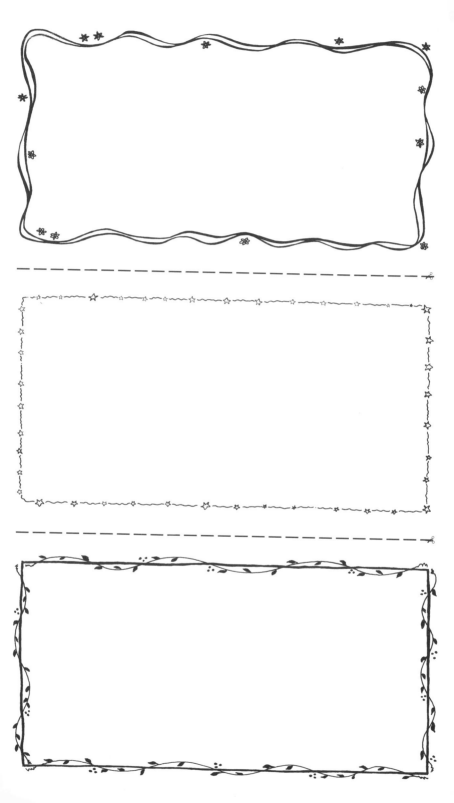

Raisin Spice Cake

1 jar Raisin Spice Cake Mix
1 C. buttermilk
1/2 C. vegetable oil

1 tsp. vanilla
2 T. rum or brandy

Preheat the oven to 350°F. Empty contents of jar into a mixing bowl, stirring to combine. Add buttermilk, oil, vanilla and rum or brandy. Stir well until the mixture is well blended. Pour batter into a greased 7 x 11 inch pan or 9 inch round pan. Bake for 35 to 40 minutes. If desired, make a frosting by whipping 1/2 C. shortening with 2 C. powdered sugar then add 1 tsp. vanilla and 3 to 4 T. milk and continue to whip until fluffy.

Raisin Spice Cake

1 jar Raisin Spice Cake Mix
1 C. buttermilk
1/2 C. vegetable oil

1 tsp. vanilla
2 T. rum or brandy

Preheat the oven to 350°F. Empty contents of jar into a mixing bowl, stirring to combine. Add buttermilk, oil, vanilla and rum or brandy. Stir well until the mixture is well blended. Pour batter into a greased 7 x 11 inch pan or 9 inch round pan. Bake for 35 to 40 minutes. If desired, make a frosting by whipping 1/2 C. shortening with 2 C. powdered sugar then add 1 tsp. vanilla and 3 to 4 T. milk and continue to whip until fluffy.

Raisin Spice Cake

1 jar Raisin Spice Cake Mix
1 C. buttermilk
1/2 C. vegetable oil

1 tsp. vanilla
2 T. rum or brandy

Preheat the oven to 350°F. Empty contents of jar into a mixing bowl, stirring to combine. Add buttermilk, oil, vanilla and rum or brandy. Stir well until the mixture is well blended. Pour batter into a greased 7 x 11 inch pan or 9 inch round pan. Bake for 35 to 40 minutes. If desired, make a frosting by whipping 1/2 C. shortening with 2 C. powdered sugar then add 1 tsp. vanilla and 3 to 4 T. milk and continue to whip until fluffy.

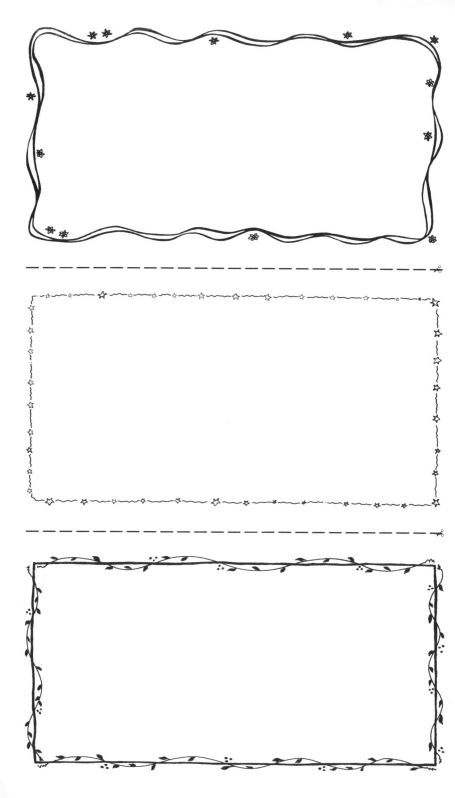

Date Nut Cake Mix

1 C. chopped walnuts
2/3 C. brown sugar
1/2 tsp. salt
1/2 tsp. baking powder
1 1/3 C. flour

1 1/4 C. dates in a baggie

Layer the ingredients in the order given into a wide-mouth 1-quart canning jar. Pack each layer into place before adding the next ingredient.

Attach a gift tag with the mixing and baking instructions.

❋ *Small appliques or embroidery can be added to the center of a fabric cover to further personalize the gift.* ❋

Date Nut Cake

1 jar Date Nut Cake Mix
1 tsp. baking soda
2 eggs
1/4 C. vegetable oil
1 tsp. vanilla

Preheat oven to 350°F. Remove dates and place in a medium bowl. Sprinkle baking soda over dates. Bring 3/4 cup of water to a boil and pour over dates. Set aside and let cool. Empty remaining ingredients into a mixing bowl, stirring to combine. Make a well in the center and add eggs, oil, vanilla and cooled date mixture. Stir until well combined. Transfer batter to a greased 7 x 11 inch pan or 9 inch round pan. Bake for 30 to 35 minutes.

Date Nut Cake

1 jar Date Nut Cake Mix
1 tsp. baking soda
2 eggs

1/4 C. vegetable oil
1 tsp. vanilla

Preheat oven to 350°F. Remove dates and place in a medium bowl. Sprinkle baking soda over dates. Bring 3/4 cup of water to a boil and pour over dates. Set aside and let cool. Empty remaining ingredients into a mixing bowl, stirring to combine. Make a well in the center and add eggs, oil, vanilla and cooled date mixture. Stir until well combined. Transfer batter to a greased 7 x 11 inch pan or 9 inch round pan. Bake for 30 to 35 minutes.

Date Nut Cake

1 jar Date Nut Cake Mix
1 tsp. baking soda
2 eggs

1/4 C. vegetable oil
1 tsp. vanilla

Preheat oven to 350°F. Remove dates and place in a medium bowl. Sprinkle baking soda over dates. Bring 3/4 cup of water to a boil and pour over dates. Set aside and let cool. Empty remaining ingredients into a mixing bowl, stirring to combine. Make a well in the center and add eggs, oil, vanilla and cooled date mixture. Stir until well combined. Transfer batter to a greased 7 x 11 inch pan or 9 inch round pan. Bake for 30 to 35 minutes.

Date Nut Cake

1 jar Date Nut Cake Mix
1 tsp. baking soda
2 eggs

1/4 C. vegetable oil
1 tsp. vanilla

Preheat oven to 350°F. Remove dates and place in a medium bowl. Sprinkle baking soda over dates. Bring 3/4 cup of water to a boil and pour over dates. Set aside and let cool. Empty remaining ingredients into a mixing bowl, stirring to combine. Make a well in the center and add eggs, oil, vanilla and cooled date mixture. Stir until well combined. Transfer batter to a greased 7 x 11 inch pan or 9 inch round pan. Bake for 30 to 35 minutes.

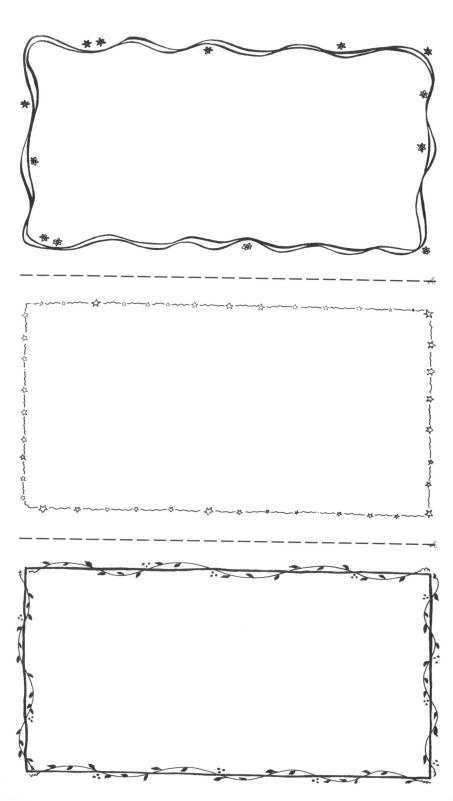

Date Nut Cake

1 jar Date Nut Cake Mix
1 tsp. baking soda
2 eggs

1/4 C. vegetable oil
1 tsp. vanilla

Preheat oven to 350°F. Remove dates and place in a medium bowl. Sprinkle baking soda over dates. Bring 3/4 cup of water to a boil and pour over dates. Set aside and let cool. Empty remaining ingredients into a mixing bowl, stirring to combine. Make a well in the center and add eggs, oil, vanilla and cooled date mixture. Stir until well combined. Transfer batter to a greased 7 x 11 inch pan or 9 inch round pan. Bake for 30 to 35 minutes.

Date Nut Cake

1 jar Date Nut Cake Mix
1 tsp. baking soda
2 eggs

1/4 C. vegetable oil
1 tsp. vanilla

Preheat oven to 350°F. Remove dates and place in a medium bowl. Sprinkle baking soda over dates. Bring 3/4 cup of water to a boil and pour over dates. Set aside and let cool. Empty remaining ingredients into a mixing bowl, stirring to combine. Make a well in the center and add eggs, oil, vanilla and cooled date mixture. Stir until well combined. Transfer batter to a greased 7 x 11 inch pan or 9 inch round pan. Bake for 30 to 35 minutes.

Date Nut Cake

1 jar Date Nut Cake Mix
1 tsp. baking soda
2 eggs

1/4 C. vegetable oil
1 tsp. vanilla

Preheat oven to 350°F. Remove dates and place in a medium bowl. Sprinkle baking soda over dates. Bring 3/4 cup of water to a boil and pour over dates. Set aside and let cool. Empty remaining ingredients into a mixing bowl, stirring to combine. Make a well in the center and add eggs, oil, vanilla and cooled date mixture. Stir until well combined. Transfer batter to a greased 7 x 11 inch pan or 9 inch round pan. Bake for 30 to 35 minutes.

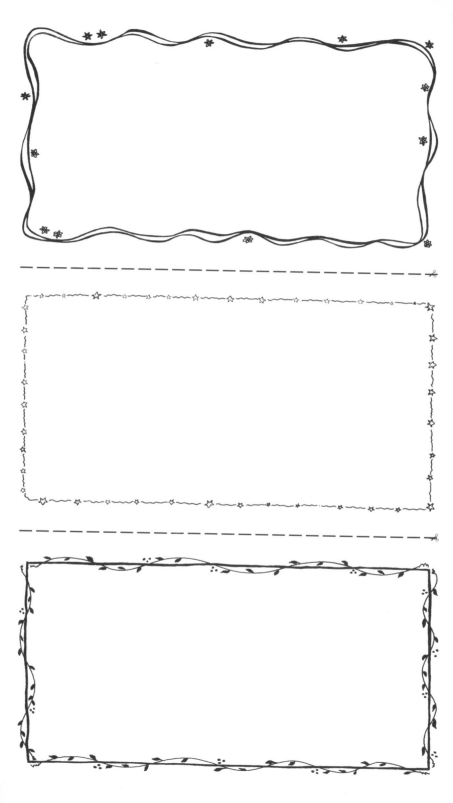

Rich Chocolate Cake Mix

2 C. sugar
1 tsp. baking soda
1/2 tsp. salt
2 C. flour

1/3 C. unsweetened cocoa in
a baggie

Layer the ingredients in the order given into a wide-mouth 1-quart canning jar. Pack each layer into place before adding the next ingredient.

Attach a gift tag with the mixing and baking instructions.

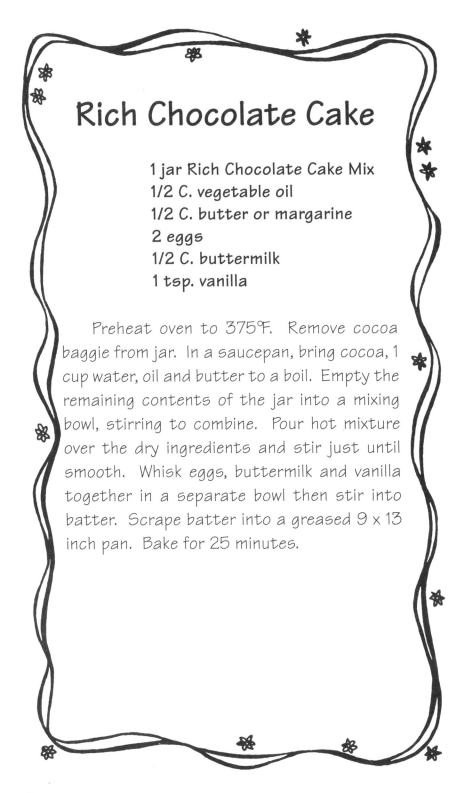

Rich Chocolate Cake

1 jar Rich Chocolate Cake Mix
1/2 C. vegetable oil
1/2 C. butter or margarine
2 eggs
1/2 C. buttermilk
1 tsp. vanilla

Preheat oven to 375°F. Remove cocoa baggie from jar. In a saucepan, bring cocoa, 1 cup water, oil and butter to a boil. Empty the remaining contents of the jar into a mixing bowl, stirring to combine. Pour hot mixture over the dry ingredients and stir just until smooth. Whisk eggs, buttermilk and vanilla together in a separate bowl then stir into batter. Scrape batter into a greased 9 x 13 inch pan. Bake for 25 minutes.

Rich Chocolate Cake

1 jar Rich Chocolate Cake Mix	2 eggs
1/2 C. vegetable oil	1/2 C. buttermilk
1/2 C. butter or margarine	1 tsp. vanilla

Preheat oven to 375°F. Remove cocoa baggie from jar. In a saucepan, bring cocoa, 1 cup water, oil and butter to a boil. Empty the remaining contents of the jar into a mixing bowl, stirring to combine. Pour hot mixture over the dry ingredients and stir just until smooth. Whisk eggs, buttermilk and vanilla together in a separate bowl then stir into batter. Scrape batter into a greased 9 x 13 inch pan. Bake for 25 minutes.

Rich Chocolate Cake

1 jar Rich Chocolate Cake Mix	2 eggs
1/2 C. vegetable oil	1/2 C. buttermilk
1/2 C. butter or margarine	1 tsp. vanilla

Preheat oven to 375°F. Remove cocoa baggie from jar. In a saucepan, bring cocoa, 1 cup water, oil and butter to a boil. Empty the remaining contents of the jar into a mixing bowl, stirring to combine. Pour hot mixture over the dry ingredients and stir just until smooth. Whisk eggs, buttermilk and vanilla together in a separate bowl then stir into batter. Scrape batter into a greased 9 x 13 inch pan. Bake for 25 minutes.

Rich Chocolate Cake

1 jar Rich Chocolate Cake Mix	2 eggs
1/2 C. vegetable oil	1/2 C. buttermilk
1/2 C. butter or margarine	1 tsp. vanilla

Preheat oven to 375°F. Remove cocoa baggie from jar. In a saucepan, bring cocoa, 1 cup water, oil and butter to a boil. Empty the remaining contents of the jar into a mixing bowl, stirring to combine. Pour hot mixture over the dry ingredients and stir just until smooth. Whisk eggs, buttermilk and vanilla together in a separate bowl then stir into batter. Scrape batter into a greased 9 x 13 inch pan. Bake for 25 minutes.

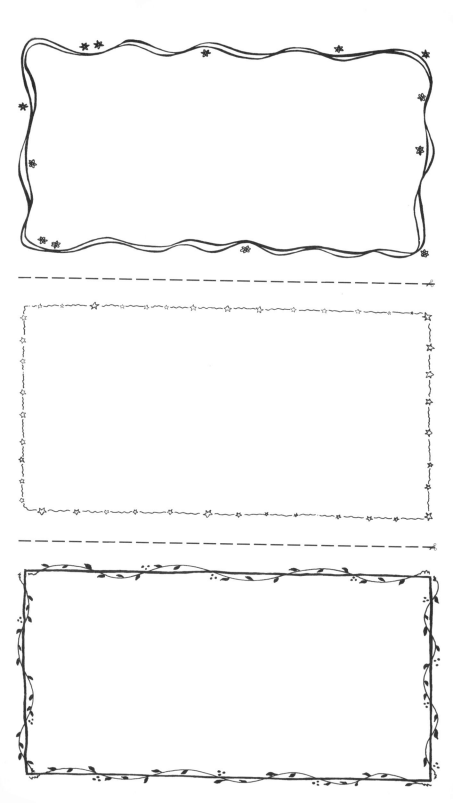

Rich Chocolate Cake

1 jar Rich Chocolate Cake Mix
1/2 C. vegetable oil
1/2 C. butter or margarine

2 eggs
1/2 C. buttermilk
1 tsp. vanilla

Preheat oven to 375°F. Remove cocoa baggie from jar. In a saucepan, bring cocoa, 1 cup water, oil and butter to a boil. Empty the remaining contents of the jar into a mixing bowl, stirring to combine. Pour hot mixture over the dry ingredients and stir just until smooth. Whisk eggs, buttermilk and vanilla together in a separate bowl then stir into batter. Scrape batter into a greased 9 x 13 inch pan. Bake for 25 minutes.

Rich Chocolate Cake

1 jar Rich Chocolate Cake Mix
1/2 C. vegetable oil
1/2 C. butter or margarine

2 eggs
1/2 C. buttermilk
1 tsp. vanilla

Preheat oven to 375°F. Remove cocoa baggie from jar. In a saucepan, bring cocoa, 1 cup water, oil and butter to a boil. Empty the remaining contents of the jar into a mixing bowl, stirring to combine. Pour hot mixture over the dry ingredients and stir just until smooth. Whisk eggs, buttermilk and vanilla together in a separate bowl then stir into batter. Scrape batter into a greased 9 x 13 inch pan. Bake for 25 minutes.

Rich Chocolate Cake

1 jar Rich Chocolate Cake Mix
1/2 C. vegetable oil
1/2 C. butter or margarine

2 eggs
1/2 C. buttermilk
1 tsp. vanilla

Preheat oven to 375°F. Remove cocoa baggie from jar. In a saucepan, bring cocoa, 1 cup water, oil and butter to a boil. Empty the remaining contents of the jar into a mixing bowl, stirring to combine. Pour hot mixture over the dry ingredients and stir just until smooth. Whisk eggs, buttermilk and vanilla together in a separate bowl then stir into batter. Scrape batter into a greased 9 x 13 inch pan. Bake for 25 minutes.

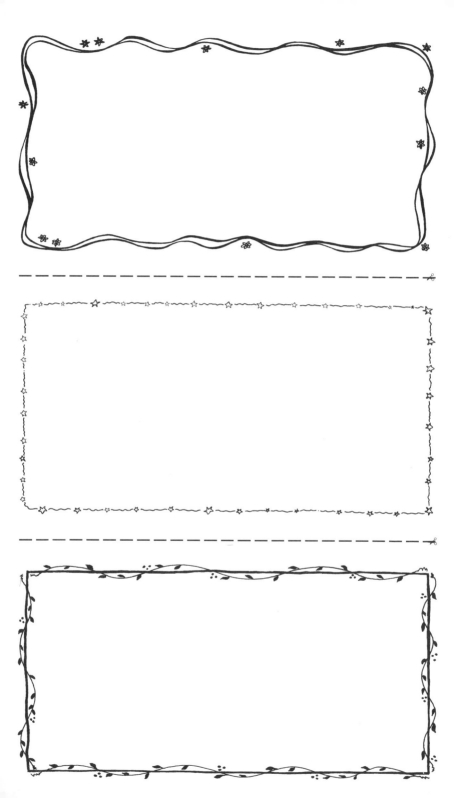

Peach Crumb Cake Mix

3/4 C. sugar
3/4 C. quick oats
3/4 C. brown sugar
2 C. flour
2 tsp. baking powder
1/2 tsp. salt

Layer the ingredients in the order given into a wide-mouth 1-quart canning jar. Pack each layer into place before adding the next ingredient.

Attach a gift tag with the mixing and baking instructions.

❀ *For a special touch, attach a wooden spoon to the jar.* ❀

Peach Crumb Cake

1 jar Peach Crumb Cake Mix
3/4 C. butter or margarine
1 (29 oz.) can peach pie filling

Preheat oven to 350°F. Empty contents of jar into a mixing bowl, stirring to combine. Melt butter and stir into dry ingredients to form a crumbly mixture. Press half of the crumbs into a greased 9 x 13 inch pan and top with peach pie filling. Sprinkle remaining crumb mixture over filling. Bake for 30 to 35 minutes.

Peach Crumb Cake

1 jar Peach Crumb Cake Mix
3/4 C. butter or margarine

1 (29 oz.) can peach pie
  filling

Preheat oven to 350°F. Empty contents of jar into a mixing bowl, stirring to combine. Melt butter and stir into dry ingredients to form a crumbly mixture. Press half of the crumbs into a greased 9 x 13 inch pan and top with peach pie filling. Sprinkle remaining crumb mixture over filling. Bake for 30 to 35 minutes.

Peach Crumb Cake

1 jar Peach Crumb Cake Mix
3/4 C. butter or margarine

1 (29 oz.) can peach pie
  filling

Preheat oven to 350°F. Empty contents of jar into a mixing bowl, stirring to combine. Melt butter and stir into dry ingredients to form a crumbly mixture. Press half of the crumbs into a greased 9 x 13 inch pan and top with peach pie filling. Sprinkle remaining crumb mixture over filling. Bake for 30 to 35 minutes.

Peach Crumb Cake

1 jar Peach Crumb Cake Mix
3/4 C. butter or margarine

1 (29 oz.) can peach pie
  filling

Preheat oven to 350°F. Empty contents of jar into a mixing bowl, stirring to combine. Melt butter and stir into dry ingredients to form a crumbly mixture. Press half of the crumbs into a greased 9 x 13 inch pan and top with peach pie filling. Sprinkle remaining crumb mixture over filling. Bake for 30 to 35 minutes.

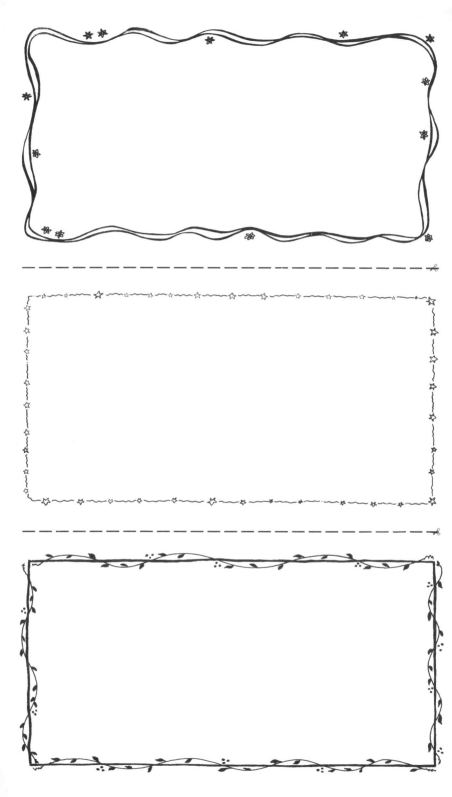

Peach Crumb Cake

1 jar Peach Crumb Cake Mix   1 (29 oz.) can peach pie
3/4 C. butter or margarine   filling

     Preheat oven to 350°F. Empty contents of jar into a mixing
bowl, stirring to combine. Melt butter and stir into dry ingredients
to form a crumbly mixture. Press half of the crumbs into a greased
9 x 13 inch pan and top with peach pie filling. Sprinkle remaining
crumb mixture over filling. Bake for 30 to 35 minutes.

Peach Crumb Cake

1 jar Peach Crumb Cake Mix   1 (29 oz.) can peach pie
3/4 C. butter or margarine   filling

     Preheat oven to 350°F. Empty contents of jar into a mixing
bowl, stirring to combine. Melt butter and stir into dry ingredients
to form a crumbly mixture. Press half of the crumbs into a greased
9 x 13 inch pan and top with peach pie filling. Sprinkle remaining
crumb mixture over filling. Bake for 30 to 35 minutes.

Peach Crumb Cake

1 jar Peach Crumb Cake Mix   1 (29 oz.) can peach pie
3/4 C. butter or margarine   filling

     Preheat oven to 350°F. Empty contents of jar into a mixing
bowl, stirring to combine. Melt butter and stir into dry ingredients
to form a crumbly mixture. Press half of the crumbs into a greased
9 x 13 inch pan and top with peach pie filling. Sprinkle remaining
crumb mixture over filling. Bake for 30 to 35 minutes.

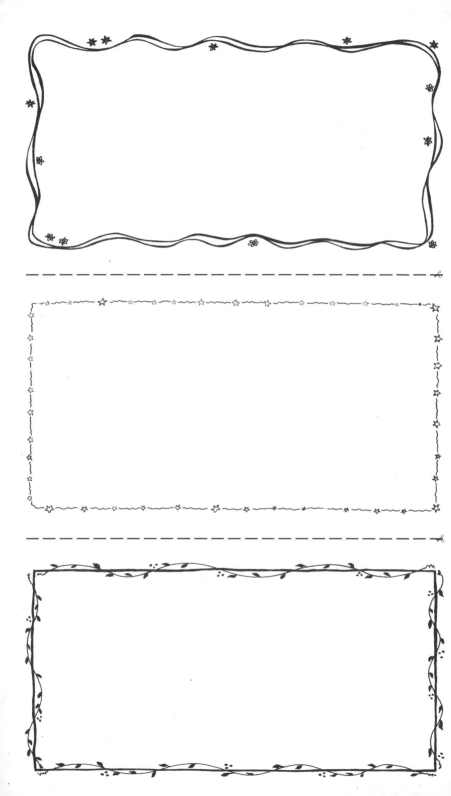